Food Culture in
Southeast Asia

Southeast Asia. Cartography by Bookcomp, Inc.

Food Culture in
Southeast Asia

PENNY VAN ESTERIK

Food Culture around the World

Ken Albala, Series Editor

GREENWOOD PRESS
Westport, Connecticut • London

Library of Congress Cataloging-in-Publication Data

Van Esterik, Penny.
  Food culture in Southeast Asia / Penny Van Esterik.
      p. cm. — (Food culture around the world, ISSN 1545–2638)
  Includes bibliographical references and index.
  ISBN 978–0–313–34419–0 (alk. paper)
  1. Cookery, Southeast Asian.   2. Food habits—Southeast Asia.   I. Title.
  TX724.5.S68V36   2008
  394.1'20959—dc22   2008020224

British Library Cataloguing in Publication Data is available.

Library of Congress Catalog Card Number: 2008020224
ISBN: 978–0–313–34419–0
ISSN: 1545–2638

First published in 2008

Greenwood Press, 88 Post Road West, Westport, CT 06881
An imprint of Greenwood Publishing Group, Inc.
www.greenwood.com

Printed in the United States of America

The paper used in this book complies with the
Permanent Paper Standard issued by the National
Information Standards Organization (Z39.48–1984).

10 9 8 7 6 5 4 3 2 1

The publisher has done its best to make sure the instructions and/or recipes in this book
are correct. However, users should apply judgment and experience when preparing recipes,
especially parents and teachers working with young people. The publisher accepts no re-
sponsibility for the outcome of any recipe included in this volume.

All photos are by the author unless otherwise noted.

In gratitude to those who fed me, taught me to cook, and ate with me—in Southeast Asia and elsewhere.

Contents

Series Foreword

The appearance of the Food Culture around the World series marks a definitive stage in the maturation of Food Studies as a discipline to reach a wider audience of students, general readers, and foodies alike. In comprehensive interdisciplinary reference volumes, each on the food culture of a country or region for which information is most in demand, a remarkable team of experts from around the world offers a deeper understanding and appreciation of the role of food in shaping human culture for a whole new generation. I am honored to have been associated with this project as series editor.

Each volume follows a series format, with a chronology of food-related dates and narrative chapters entitled Introduction, Historical Overview, Major Foods and Ingredients, Cooking, Typical Meals, Eating Out, Special Occasions, and Diet and Health. (In special cases, these topics are covered by region.) Each also includes a glossary, bibliography, resource guide, and illustrations.

Finding or growing food has of course been the major preoccupation of our species throughout history, but how various peoples around the world learn to exploit their natural resources, come to esteem or shun specific foods and develop unique cuisines reveals much more about what it is to be human. There is perhaps no better way to understand a culture, its values, preoccupations and fears, than by examining its attitudes toward food. Food provides the daily sustenance around which families and communities bond. It provides the material basis for rituals through which people celebrate the passage of life stages and their connection to divinity. Food preferences also serve to separate individuals and groups from each other, and as one of the most powerful factors in the construction of identity, we physically, emotionally and spiritually become what we eat.

By studying the foodways of people different from ourselves we also grow to understand and tolerate the rich diversity of practices around the world. What seems strange or frightening among other people becomes perfectly rational when set in context. It is my hope that readers will gain from these volumes not only an aesthetic appreciation for the glories of the many culinary traditions described, but also ultimately a more profound respect for the peoples who devised them. Whether it is eating New Year's dumplings in China, folding tamales with friends in Mexico, or going out to a famous Michelin-starred restaurant in France, understanding these food traditions helps us to understand the people themselves.

As globalization proceeds apace in the twenty-first century it is also more important than ever to preserve unique local and regional traditions. In many cases these books describe ways of eating that have already begun to disappear or have been seriously transformed by modernity. To know how and why these losses occur today also enables us to decide what traditions, whether from our own heritage or that of others, we wish to keep alive. These books are thus not only about the food and culture of peoples around the world, but also about ourselves and who we hope to be.

Ken Albala
University of the Pacific

Preface

I don't think of myself as a food writer but instead as a nutritional anthropologist who writes about both food and Southeast Asia. It is difficult to work in the region and not write about food because that is what is important to Southeast Asians and, thus, should be equally important to analysts. I came to know Southeast Asia through its food—first Thai food in the 1960s then Lao and Malay food in the 1990s, interspersed with tastes of Burma, Cambodia, and Vietnam. I am acutely aware of the need for more research in the latter countries before broader connections to island Southeast Asia can be made in future publications.

The most difficult problem I faced in writing this book, other than selecting what foods and meals to feature, was removing my food voice from the story. For food is an intensely personal product, deeply embedded in senses and memories. Forty years ago, chiles were terrifying irritants that threatened my adjustment to Thailand; now they are an addiction. I recall my trepidation the first time I purchased food from street vendors, having been told to expect dirty, unpleasant food, and finding only tasty and safe creations. The only time I had a seriously upset stomach in Thailand, caused by what the Thai call an "eating mistake" (*kin phit*), was when I craved Western food and ate in high-end hotels. Unlike many food writers on Southeast Asia, several of my experiences come from eating in village homes and temples. For me, the smell of chiles and garlic hitting the oil and the thump of mortar and pestle early in the morning as women prepared flavor pastes, will forever signal rural village mornings. I hope this book captures something of the range of meals in the region, from padi fields to palaces.

Acknowledgments

I owe a great debt of gratitude to the unnamed and unknown cooks whose food I ate in markets, street stalls, and restaurants throughout the region, particularly to those who didn't assume they had to adjust the spices for a foreigner. I am very grateful to Naomi Duguid for advice on food and recipe writing, Lisa Drummond for her expertise on Vietnam, Thanes Wongyannava and Kanit Muntarbhorn for sharing with me their historical research on Thai food, and the staff of the WABA (World Alliance for Breastfeeding Action) secretariat in Penang for introducing me to Malay food. My greatest debt is to my husband John, whose knowledge of Southeast Asia informs every chapter.

Thanks to my recipe tasters and testers including Fred and Anne Grant; Julie Martin and Leo, Dylan, and Tim Posgate; Garth Elliot; Fran Grant; Karen Whitewood; Barb Hopkins; Pam and Wayne Somers; Vera and Ainslie Yellery; Cynthia Webster; Ken Little; Teresa Holmes; Daphne Winland; Steve Gaetz; Naomi and Sophie Adelson; Albert Schrauwers; and David Murray.

I'm grateful to my Greenwood editor, Wendi Schnaufer, for her excellent problem-solving skills and overall support, and to Ken Albala for persuading me to take on what seemed like an impossible task—writing this book.

Introduction

Southeast Asia was known to the ancient Greeks as the Golden Khersonese, the "golden peninsula" lying east of India and south of China, tapering off into hundreds of islands to the south, best known to us as Indonesia and the Philippines. Today, as in the past, the peninsula acts as a barrier and a bridge between India and China, as it lies across trade routes between those two more populous and powerful regions to the east and north. "Golden" refers to the wealth locals and sojourners derived from Southeast Asia's strategic position across trade routes.

Outsiders have defined Southeast Asia as Further India or Greater India—the Indian subcontinent on a smaller scale; geographers called it Asia of the Monsoons; farther west, terms like Little China or Indochina stressed connections with China. All these terms deprecate the important individuality of the region. In the Second World War, the allied forces labeled the space between India and China the Southeast Asian theater of war.[1]

Historical sources suggest that Southeast Asians themselves made no use of a regional category like Southeast Asia. Thus, there is no record of an indigenous concept that we can conveniently borrow to avoid using colonial, military, or imperialist terminology. Instead, we must make use of the configuration and label that originates from colonial officials, missionaries, the military, and western visitors, just as the nations of Southeast Asia do today, but with awareness of the layers of history behind the name. The term is useful because it enables us to see continuities as well as diversities across this vast area—enough to recommend using the term and even searching out commonalities in food culture in the region.

Perhaps the most notable feature of Southeast Asia is its diversity—in ecologies, languages, ethnicities, religions, and political systems. Then how can we hope to characterize its food culture? For the purpose of this book, we focus on the food of the countries of mainland Southeast Asia, using Malaysia as a transition to brief comparisons, where possible, with the island cuisines of Indonesia and the Philippines.

LANDS AND NATIONS

Southeast Asia has a combined land area of 4,609,048 square kilometers (1,783,426 sq mi)[2] and stretches over 3,500 miles west to east. But it is the sea that dominates the region around the waters of the Sunda shelf—a shallow sea (only 120 feet deep) stretching from the Gulf of Thailand to Borneo and Java, connecting the mainland to island Southeast Asia around 18,000 years ago. This land bridge facilitated the movements of people from the mainland into the islands of Southeast Asia and explains why the mainland and the islands form a unit with shared flora and fauna. Many cultural continuities existing between the mainland and the islands are most clearly seen when comparing Malaysia with the island of Sumatra.

Southeast Asia today consists of the mainland countries of Burma (Myanmar), Thailand, Lao People's Democratic Republic (Lao PDR), Vietnam, Cambodia, and Malaysia, and the island countries of Singapore, Brunei, East Timor, Indonesia, and the Philippines. Malaysia represents a transitional zone; the mainland peninsula is technically part of mainland Southeast Asia, but parts of East Malaysia are on the island of Borneo. The Ring of Fire, an area of earthquake action and active volcanoes, stretches from Burma across the Sunda shelf into Indonesia and the Philippines. Most of mainland Southeast Asia is an area of stable geological structures although not entirely immune to volcanic activity. The 2004 tsunami caused by an earthquake off Sumatra killed at least 270,000 and displaced over a million and a half people. Indonesia, Thailand, and East Malaysia were the most affected countries in Southeast Asia.

Malaysia and Singapore were one nation until 1965 when Singapore became an island financial powerhouse. Political systems vary widely: There are countries ruled by military dictatorships (Burma), constitutional monarchies (Thailand, Malaysia, Brunei), socialist or communist regimes (Lao PDR, Vietnam), and republics (Indonesia, the Philippines).

Thailand takes pride in celebrating the longest-ruling monarch in the world, the present King Bhumibol Aduladej.

HILL FARMS AND PADI FIELDS

Southeast Asia is characterized by a series of significant contrasts—mainland and island, upland and lowland, inland and coastal, palace and village, wet rice and root crops, dry rice and irrigated rice—contrasts that help to organize the diversity of ethnic groups, languages, political systems, and religions in the region.[3]

The most basic division in Southeast Asia separates mainland from island; the mainland is dominated by rivers with highlands separating the river valleys, while island Southeast Asia is oriented around the sea as a means for communication. Large agricultural civilizations based on wet-rice agriculture grew up in the river delta areas of the mainland—the Chao Phraya in Central Thailand; the Irrawaddy River in Burma; the Mekong River in Lao PDR, Thailand, Cambodia, and Vietnam; and the Red River in North Vietnam, as well as special zones like the area around the Tonle Sap in the Cambodian basin. Civilizations on the islands of Southeast Asia were based around control of the sea-lanes and developed on islands such as Java, Sumatra, and Bali.

Another contrast stresses the relation between the small-scale agriculture of the uplands and the agriculturally based kingdoms of the great river valleys. The rugged mountains, only rarely above 6,000 feet, can hinder communication across upland regions and with the lowlands. For example, in Sumatra a mountain range inhibits cross-island communication. The upland peoples often practice shifting (swidden) cultivation; fields are cleared, burned for fertilizer, planted, harvested, and left to fallow while the subsistence farmers shift to plant new fields. Between uplands and the lowland river valleys, the Shan Plateau at 4,000 feet and the Khorat Plateau at 1,000 feet provide different agricultural opportunities, including the use of foothills for fruit orchards.

Rice, the dominant staple of Southeast Asia, adapts to different ecological niches, and creates new niches such as the rice terraces of Bali and Ifugao province in the Philippines. The most basic contrasts in rice distinguish between dry- and wet-rice cultivation, and in the mainland, between those who grow and eat glutinous or sticky rice and those who prefer the non-glutinous varieties. A more ancient contrast distinguishes ancient root cropping areas from rice growing areas.

Within each region, an additional contrast separates the royal court centers from the outlying rural peripheries. These contrasts shape the

Rice terraces in Banaue, Ifugao Province, Philippines, 2000. Courtesy of B. Lynne Milgram.

food culture in Southeast Asia and are reflected in the meals and recipes described in this book.

The lowlands had greater language unity, more political unity, easier transport, and cultivated wet rice. The uplands in both mainland and islands were characterized by linguistic diversity, subsistence swidden cultivation, lower population density, and more political fragmentation.

CLIMATE

Southeast Asia generally has a tropical forest climate. Most of the mainland has three seasons—cool (November–February), hot (March–May), and rainy (June–October). There are some differences with regard to temperature and precipitation between the mainland and the islands; some parts of mainland Southeast Asia get colder temperatures and droughts. The islands of Southeast Asia have generally higher temperatures and heavier rains. The influence of low rainfall in some areas like upper Burma and the Khorat Plateau in northeastern Thailand affected the growth and decline of populations and civilizations. The dry soil in these areas, leached of nutrients, was used for building bricks (laterite) for temples and monuments.

Southeast Asian climate is related to the action of the monsoons. Monsoon winds bring high humidity and heavy rainfall. From March to October the southwest monsoon comes over the Indian Ocean, picking up moisture and dumping it on southwest-facing coasts for those months. From October to January the northeast monsoon winds pick up moisture from the South China Sea and dump rain on northeast-facing coasts. Thus some parts of mainland Southeast Asia do have variations in rainfall and can suffer droughts, while much of island Southeast Asia receives rainfall more or less continuously throughout the year. For example, much of the Malay Peninsula has no dry season.

The differences in climate within Southeast Asia have resulted in variations in forest cover; some areas have heavy tropical rainforests, while others have some seasonal forest cover. The types of forests characteristic of parts of Burma and Thailand favor teak production, but teak is unavailable in those countries today. Heavy use of forest products, excessive logging, and decreasing fallow time for swidden agriculture over the past 50 years have severely reduced forest cover in most of Southeast Asia, resulting in heavy floods and serious pollution of rivers, compromising the use of rivers for drinking water, swimming, and fishing. For example, Thailand had about 70% forest cover in the 1960s and has about 17% today. Lao PDR has the heaviest forest cover in Southeast Asia but recently has seen dramatic declines in forest cover. Throughout Southeast Asia, forests have provided a significant amount of food. In particular, bamboo forests provide housing and basketry materials as well as food.

WATER

Water shaped Southeast Asia; oceans and seas form its borders, and great rivers draining from northern mountains flow north to south from Tibet and China, flooding the lowlands of the mainland countries. These mainland river valleys were the routes for people moving into Southeast Asia more than a thousand years ago—the ancestors of the Burmese moving down the Irrawaddy and Salween rivers; the ancestors of the Thai moving down the Mekong and Chao Phraya rivers; and the ancestors of the Vietnamese moving down the Red River valley. The Mekong River and its delta in southern Vietnam is the longest river in Southeast Asia, forming boundaries and bounty for communities living in south China, Thailand, Lao PDR, Cambodia, and Vietnam.

These rivers and their tributaries create rich alluvial soils ideally suited for wet-rice agriculture. In Cambodia, the great Tonle Sap Lake represents the largest reserve of freshwater fish in the world during the rainy season. The Khmer built their earliest civilizations around the Mekong River and the Tonle Sap.

Sea-borne commerce was important to both mainland and island Southeast Asia. Control of straits and portage routes such as the Isthmus of Kra would mean wealth and the concentration of political power through trade—particularly important for the early civilizations in Sumatra and the Malay Peninsula, and the expansion of trading ports such as Malacca and Singapore.

PEOPLES OF SOUTHEAST ASIA

The people of Southeast Asia are as diverse as the geographies they occupy. Although there are pockets of dense population, such as in Java, for most of history population density was low, and wars sought control of people, not land, moving prisoners of war from place to place.

All the countries of Southeast Asia are plural societies characterized by a dominant ethnic majority and a varying number of ethnic minorities with complex and historical linkages among them. For example, the Burmans in Burma represent about 68% of the population; the Thai in Thailand, around 75%; the Lao in Lao PDR, 68%; the Khmer in Cambodia, around 90%; the Vietnamese in Vietnam, 85–90%, and the Malay in Malaysia, 58%. In Malaysia, the Chinese are a numerical minority (26%) in a system of managed multiculturalism. Singapore, after breaking off from Muslim Malaysia in 1965, maintains its ethnic balance of around 75% Chinese, 15% Malay, and 7% Indian, giving Chinese Singaporeans numerical and political dominance. Javanese make up 45% of the population of Indonesia, and in the Philippines, the population is composed of over 90% Christian Malays.[4] Vietnam is the most Sinicized country in Southeast Asia; the Philippines, the most Christian; and Indonesia, the most populous Muslim country in the world.

Most countries in Southeast Asia have sizable Chinese and Indian minorities, a legacy of trading patterns and European colonization. A recent publication estimates that about 80% of all overseas Chinese live in Southeast Asia.[5] Chinese and Indian minorities are often the most economically powerful merchants in urban Southeast Asia.

Defining who is a minority is a constantly changing political act. The Lao government, for example, recognizes 65 distinct ethnic groups but stresses "unity in diversity" among them all. Figures always represent how the government wants to define ethnic minorities and dominant ethnic groups. Ethnic minorities such as the Karen, Akha, and Hmong cross national borders, while other groups such as the Lisu, Chin, Kachin, and

Semang occupy marginal lands such as dense upland forests. Most ethnic minorities are adapted to upland mountain ecologies. The historic importance of upland peoples is reflected in their interdependence with lowland groups, often expressed in rituals acknowledging their status as the original inhabitants of the land.

LANGUAGE FAMILIES

The ethnic diversity in Southeast Asia is created by and reflected in its linguistic diversity. While there are national languages and more linguistic homogeneity in the lowland plains than in the hills, the languages in Southeast Asia come from many distinct language families. Although there are some disagreements among linguists about the classification of some languages (including Vietnamese, Karen, and Hmong), there is agreement that there are at least four major families of languages spoken in Southeast Asia, including Sino-Tibetan, Austro-Asiatic, Austronesian, and Tai-Kadai. The Sino-Tibetan language family includes speakers of Chinese, Burmese, Chin, and Kachin. The Austro-Asiatic family includes Mon and Khmer (Cambodian). The Tai-Kadai language family includes Thai, Lao, and Shan. Austronesian language families include small numbers of speakers of Cham and Rhade, and large numbers of Malay, Tagalog, and Indonesian speakers.

The dominant national languages in mainland Southeast Asia are tonal. For example, Thai has five tones. Burmese, Thai, Lao, and Cambodian scripts are based on Indic scripts, and Pali-Sanskrit loan words are common, particularly in matters of religion (Buddhism) and law. French colonial missionaries worked out a Roman transcription for Vietnamese to replace Chinese-based scripts. Where there were great royal courts, languages developed complex systems of honorifics and different language levels for maintaining systems of social hierarchy. For example, pronouns differ depending whether one is addressing royalty, elders, teachers, friends of the same age, children, or servants. This can be clearly demonstrated with the Thai verb *to eat*, a key concern of this book. *Rapathaan* is a more formal and elegant term than *thaan*, and *gin* is an everyday term used with friends and children.[6] These language levels have been removed in Lao to reflect socialist solidarity and the end of the monarchy, and are rapidly fading in importance in other languages.

National language policies have influenced the distribution of languages today. Over the last century, Central Thai replaced Northern Thai and Lao in Thailand, and majority lowland languages are often taught in upland schools in Thailand and Lao PDR.

KINSHIP, ETHNICITY, AND RELIGION

The basic form of social organization in Southeast Asia is the household, organized flexibly for rice production. The Thai word for family, *krop krua*, means literally the group that surrounds the hearth. Most Southeast Asians trace their descent through both the mother's and father's side of the family, following a form of bilateral or cognatic kinship; ideally, both males and females enjoy equal inheritance rights. In rice-growing mainland communities there is often a matrilocal bias, with husbands marrying in to their wives' household or community. It is common to adopt or foster children. In fact, kinship is established through the provision of food; those who eat together are related through food. The word *liang* in Thai and Lao (and related terms in other mainland languages) refers to the support and care of others through the provision of food.[7]

Other systems favor descent through the male line or female line, producing larger corporate groups such as lineages and clans. Many upland minorities have patrilineal clan systems that facilitate village movement and defense. The Minangkabau of Sumatra are matrilineal; they trace their descent through women. In matrilineal systems, as in most bilateral systems, the women reside close to their own relatives, inherit land, and have important ritual and practical roles in rice production, and therefore have greater autonomy and power than in patrilineal systems, where women move to live under the authority of the husband's household and clan, as in Vietnam and among many upland minorities. As a result of the importance of women in rice production, their skills in managing money, and their marketing expertise, they are viewed as having higher status than women in south and east Asia. Divinities associated with rice and the earth are feminine, and women's association with nurture are reflected in their complex relationship to food and feeding.

Theravada Buddhism is the dominant religion in the countries of mainland Southeast Asia (Burma, Thailand, Lao PDR, and Cambodia). Islam is the state religion in Brunei and Malaysia, and the religious practice of most Indonesians. Most Filipinos are Christian. Apart from these dominant traditions, there are many different religions practiced in Vietnam and among the upland minority groups. While minority upland groups are often referred to as animists who practice ancestor worship, respect for spirits and ancestors is a part of everyday religious practice for most Southeast Asians.

SOURCES AND LIMITATIONS

European and North American scholarship on Southeast Asia as a region is recent and scanty compared to what is known about Europe. In

Asian studies, the amount of scholarship on India and China far exceeded work on Southeast Asia. Anthropology is emerging as the discipline best suited to examine the diversity and distinctiveness of Southeast Asia as a region. The failure to pay regard to Southeast Asia in its own right is reflected in the early writings of archaeologists and historians who defined the cultural traits of Southeast Asia as derivative, always coming from somewhere else—primarily from China or India.

Before 1500, Chinese histories were the best source of information about Southeast Asia. Marco Polo brought knowledge of Southeast Asia to Europeans, and his report—*The Travels of Marco Polo* (1298)— contains some of the earliest clues about food and meals of Southeast Asia.

Local and translated cookbooks for internal and external audiences have been important sources for this book, but they are very recent developments. The practice of publishing cremation books in Thailand has provided some evidence of family recipes. But in general, family recipes seldom specified quantities, and stressed the importance of individual preferences and taste rather than replicability of recipes.

Biases in coverage are inevitable in a vast region covered by one short book. The bias toward the mainland is deliberate, but there is a further bias toward the better-known food cultures of the region represented by Thai and Vietnamese cuisines, growing in popularity in the global community and the subject of readily available cookbooks translated into English. Materials on Lao, Burmese, and Cambodian food are rare. Malay food is most often described in relation to Indonesian food. There is a further bias in that the food and meals discussed here are most often characteristic of lowland groups, the dominant majorities in their respective countries, rather than the minority groups in the hills. This reflects a third bias toward rice-based meals rather than root-crop-based meals, and toward the food culture of the food secure rather than the food insecure.

CULINARY CONTINUITIES AND DISCONTINUITIES: VARIATIONS ON A THEME

Southeast Asia as a region or culture area has been called a colonial construction, merely lines on a map that served imperial realities and continues to serve academics who narrowly specialize in orientalist study of one or more countries within the region. This book argues that Southeast Asia as a region has an integrity beyond its arbitrarily drawn national borders.

This introduction has provided some possible "cuts" through Southeast Asia that cross national boundaries—by geographical contrasts of upland/lowland or coastal/mountain, by language family, by ethnicity, or by religion. Each of these "cuts" shows new linkages and new ways to think about the people who inhabit Southeast Asia. In this book, we will take a culinary cut through the region, mapping similarities and differences in the way people feed themselves and the value they place on eating as a material, social, and symbolic act. We must be prepared for the possibility that food culture may not map neatly on to other cuts like religion or ethnicity. Even considering the ecological diversity in the region, the same food shed may not produce the same food culture. Our task will be to look for ways that distinct food cultures relate to one another. Will similarities in cooking or cuisine show continuity across ethnic groups or across religious differences?

Culinary continuities and discontinuities are the subject of this book. But considering the complexity and diversity of the 11 countries of Southeast Asia, how can we begin to characterize its food culture? As in other places, daily food practices shape and are shaped by local communities. But throughout Southeast Asia, the capacity to feed others by sponsoring rice meals, ceremonies, and feasts is a means of acquiring prestige and status. To anticipate the food stories in the following chapters of the book, we can make a few preliminary generalizations to orient the reader:

- Words translated as "to eat" really mean "to eat rice" in most Southeast Asian languages.
- Rice is served from a common pot with people taking individual servings on separate plates, bowls, or leaves.
- Rice is eaten with a variety of side dishes including fish, vegetables, soups, sauces, and condiments.
- In towns and cities, fork and spoon have been used for many centuries; some groups eat with clean hands (considered cleaner than forks).
- Chopsticks are only used for noodles and for Chinese meals outside of their regular use in Vietnam.

As we move across national borders, up and down mountains, and in and out of palaces and villages, a few foods may be identified that are especially useful for marking ethnic identity—an identity often formed by contrasts such as glutinous rice versus non-glutinous or ordinary rice; fish sauce versus salt; and as in all food systems, the often disparaged food of marginalized groups and minorities compared to that of the dominant majority.

MARKET NOODLES

Across Southeast Asia, in the early mornings, near workplaces, in night markets, people enjoy bowls of noodle soup. But the nature of the broth, the kind of noodles, what the vendor adds, and how customers personalize their dishes reveals the heart of food culture of Southeast Asia—the tension between culinary commonality, local diversity in the region, and personal taste preferences. A Burmese, Thai, Lao, Khmer, Vietnamese, or Malay vendor might ask the customer:

- Would you have narrow or wide noodles?
- Would you like them wet or dry or fried?
- With or without fish balls? Ground pork? Chicken? Shrimp?

For wet noodles, the vendor would add the freshest greens and herbs to a distinctive broth. After customers received their bowl of noodle soup, they would further personalize their noodles from a range of wet and dry condiments. Depending whether the vendor was located in Burma or Vietnam, Thailand or Malaysia, the wet condiments might include:

- soy sauce
- fish sauce
- hot chile sauce
- Maggi or Golden Mountain sauce
- vinegar with chiles
- lime juice or lime slices

And from the dry assortment of condiments, customers could further adjust the taste with:

- sugar
- salt
- pepper
- ginger in lime
- chopped peanuts
- dried shrimp
- fried garlic
- dried chiles

Each noodle dish is prepared to individual taste by the vendor, and further personalized by the customer with the addition of wet and dry condiments. Market noodles illustrate the range of taste choices available in even the most modest Southeast Asian market, within a common shared meal pattern. While this book examines the food culture of Southeast Asia, at the same time it also raises questions about the relationship between North American food culture and the food culture of Southeast Asia under rapidly changing conditions of globalization.

NOTES

1. Milton Osborne, *Southeast Asia: An Introductory History*, 8th ed. (St. Leonards, Australia: Allen & Unwin, 2000), p. 40.

2. C. Tweddel and L. Kimball, *Introduction to the Peoples and Cultures of Asia* (Englewood Cliffs, NJ: Prentice Hall, 1985), p. 266.

3. The title of this section, "Hill Farms and Padi Fields," is the title of Robbins Burling's 1965 book on Southeast Asia, one of the first books to stress the contrasts that characterize Southeast Asia.

4. Clark Neher, *Southeast Asia: Crossroads of the World* (DeKalb, IL: Center for Southeast Asian Studies, 2000), p. 12.

5. Leo Suryadinata, *Understanding the Ethnic Chinese in Southeast Asia* (Singapore: Institute of Southeast Asian Studies, 2007).

6. R. Scupin, *Peoples and Cultures of Asia* (Upper Saddle River, NJ: Prentice Hall, 2006), p. 338.

7. I have written about this process by attending to the way nurture is conceptualized in Southeast Asia. See, for example, Penny Van Esterik, "Nurturance and Reciprocity in Thai Studies," in *State Power and Culture in Thailand*, monograph 44, ed. P. Durrenberger, Yale Southeast Asian Studies (New Haven, CT: Yale University, 1996), pp. 22–46. See also Monica Janowski and F. Kerlogue, eds., *Kinship and Food in South East Asia* (Copenhagen: NIAS Press, 2007).

Timeline

c. 10,000 B.C.	Hunter-gatherers in Southeast Asia subsist on roots, wild plants, hunting wild animals, and fishing in fresh and salt water. People use a cultural complex of stone tools.
c. 3000	The beginnings of plant and animal domestication in Southeast Asia include the domestication of rice, pigs, dogs, and chickens. Archaeological sites from the period show evidence of pottery and metallurgy, including bronze.
c. 500	Widespread evidence for wet-rice farming using water buffalo and iron implements.
c. 100 B.C.	Dongson ritual complex widespread in region, including large bronze drums.
100 A.D.	The appearance of large ceremonial centers with moats, initial contact with Indian traders and Buddhist and Hindu religious specialists.
200–600	Appearance of the first "Indianized" kingdoms, including Funan in Cambodia and Champa in central and southern Vietnam.
800	The founding of the Khmer kingdom of Angkor, a complex of Indianized states that continues for several hundred years until the fifteenth century based

	on intensive irrigated wet-rice cultivation. Known for magnificent temple cities including Angkor Wat and Angkor Thom, built in the vicinity of the Great Lake (Tonle Sap).
1200	Mongols who have conquered China threaten mainland Southeast Asia and put pressure on the Indianized kingdoms. In 1254 Kublai Khan captures Nanchao, a Tai kingdom in southern China, and destroys Pagan, a Burmese kingdom of the upper Irrawaddy in Burma in 1256.
1289	Ramkhamheng of Sukhotai inscribes the first example of written Thai declaring his kingdom's independence from Angkor and celebrating "rice in the fields and fish in the water."
1353	Siamese from Ayuttaya first invade Angkor.
1511	The Portuguese take Malacca to increase their control of the spice trade.
1600	The English East India Company is chartered and expands spice trade.
1602	The Netherlands East India Company (VOC) is chartered. Batavia founded to control spice trade.
1600s–1700s	Spanish galleon trade between Mexico and Manila trades Mexican silver for Chinese silk and porcelain and facilitates the Columbian Exchange of food crops—such as chile peppers, corn, and tomatoes—between the regions.
1800s	The British control Burma and the Malay Peninsula, and the French form the Indochinese Union, combining Vietnam, Cambodia, and Laos into a colony.
1898	The United States defeats Spain and takes control of the Philippines.
1941–1945	The Second World War comes to Southeast Asia with the Japanese defeating the British, Dutch, and Americans to take the Philippines, Indonesia, the Malay Straits, and Burma. The Japanese declare the Greater East Asia Co-Prosperity Sphere.
1945	The war ends and many former colonies of Southeast Asia seek independence.

1946	The Philippines is independent.
1948	Burma is independent at the same time as the British end their empire in India.
1949	Indonesia defeats the Dutch and declares independence.
1953	Cambodia is independent under the leadership of Prince Sihanouk, who was the Cambodian king under the French but now becomes the country's first Prime Minister.
1954	The French leave the rest of the Indochinese Union after suffering defeat at the hands of Ho Chi Minh's forces. Vietnam is divided into two halves, the north ruled by the communists under Ho Chi Minh, the south under President Ngo Dinh Diem.
1957	Malaysia (with Singapore) gains independence after a prolonged period when British forces fought communist insurgents in the Malay jungles in a war known as the "emergency."
1963	Singapore becomes independent of Malaysia under Lee Kuan Yew.
1964	First Thai restaurant in North America opened at the Thai Pavilion at the World's Fair in Flushing, New York.
1967	The Association of Southeast Asian Nations (ASEAN) forms as a peace pact and trade organization.
1975	Communist forces take over in South Vietnam, Cambodia, and Laos.
	Flows of refugees from the communist countries of Southeast Asia—Laos, Cambodia, and Vietnam—begin. Many are resettled in Europe, the United States, Canada, and Australia.
1979	Khmer Rouge in Cambodia, who are said to have killed from one to two million of their countrymen, are driven into the jungles of western Cambodia by an invasion from Vietnam.
1980s	Expansion of Southeast Asian restaurants to the West comes with the flow of refugees from the region. At

the same time western fast food chains expand into Southeast Asia.

1997   The financial collapse of Southeast Asia is precipitated by the devaluation of the Thai currency, the baht. European food conglomerates such as Tesco and Carre Four take advantage and rapidly expand into Southeast Asia.

2004   A tsunami devastates northern Sumatra and parts of Thailand's and Malaysia's west coasts, killing 270,000 people and displacing many more.

2008   Cyclone Nargis hits Burma with more than 134,000 dead or missing and presumed dead, resulting in widespread hunger and anticipated food shortages in the future.

1

Historical Overview

Knowledge about the history of Southeast Asia comes from varied sources—first from Chinese travelers writing about their adventures, and later from colonial archaeologists interested in ancient inscriptions, texts, and monuments. Other sources include reports of Southeast Asia in the Arabic press from the late colonial period.[1]

More recently there has been access to the work of national historians in the region as well as a smattering of western historians specializing in Southeast Asian history. The picture is far from complete and changes continuously as national historians reveal colonial biases in the stories westerners told about their lands. Of course, local and national histories also change as a result of new political philosophies, as the recent histories of Lao People's Democratic Republic (Lao PDR), Cambodia, and Vietnam reveal.

This chapter reviews the archaeological and historical evidence concerning the past of mainland Southeast Asia, with emphasis on the Indianized kingdoms of the mainland and the influence of the spice trade on subsequent European colonization. This sets the foundation for the processes of globalization that is visible in contemporary Southeast Asia today.

ARCHAEOLOGICAL EVIDENCE

Southeast Asia has been populated for a very long time. Early hominid forms known as Homo erectus were found in island Southeast Asia dating from between 800,000 and 300,000 years ago. It is likely that these ancient human cousins that spread across Eurasia were not our direct ancestors. But in 2003, scientists discovered a small prehuman fossil in Indonesia and identified it as a new species with a more advanced brain structure than Homo erectus—Homo floresiensis. By one million years ago, scattered stone tools provided further evidence of occupation by ancestral humans. By 40,000 years ago, our direct ancestors, Homo sapiens, had reached the islands of Southeast Asia.

Following the end of the Pleistocene 10,000 years ago, modern Homo sapiens populations migrated south from present day China into mainland Southeast Asia and populated what are now the islands of Southeast Asia. Coastal resources and rich monsoon vegetation probably sustained successful hunting and gathering groups for thousands of years in both mainland and island sites. Much of the evidence from these coastal sites is lost to archaeologists.

Hoabhinian is the name used to refer to the hunting, gathering, and fishing peoples moving in small bands and living in caves in what is now Vietnam, Burma, and Thailand. They left behind evidence of pebble and flake tools used to exploit forest and coastal resources. Later, with ground stone tools, bone implements, pottery, and domesticated plants, small bands coexisted in different ecological niches with distinct economies, subsisting on wild plants, fish, reptiles, turtles, mollusks, shellfish, wild pigs, and cattle.

Evidence suggests that wild ancestors of rice were first cultivated in southern China around 5000 B.C. and spread rapidly into suitable niches in Southeast Asia. However, there are wild varieties of rice found on the mainland, and there may well be multiple places where rice began to be cultivated.

The small rock shelter of Spirit Cave in northern Thailand housed a population of people around 9000 B.C. who collected food such as shellfish, deer, monkey, fruit, gourds, candlenut, and betel nuts, a popular stimulant chewed throughout the region. They may possibly have gathered wild beans and peas, but there is no evidence of rice. The site was occupied between 11,000 and 5500 B.C. Hoabhinian polished stone tools were found in the upper layers.[2]

The Southeast Asian Neolithic period provides some evidence of root and fruit crop horticulture and domesticated chicken, pig, and dog. By 3000 B.C. wet-rice agriculture was established in the plains of Southeast Asia. By around 2300 B.C. there were settled villages in northeastern Thailand where people raised rice in permanent villages, domesticated water buffalo, and developed bronze technology. The site of Ban Chiang is particularly exciting since it provides evidence of both bronze and iron technology, in addition to extremely beautiful painted pottery. These vessels, along with food offerings, accompanied burials.

Dongson culture, named after a site in northern Vietnam, displayed a sophisticated bronze technological complex best known for large bronze drums decorated with elaborate geometric and representational designs, including symbols for rice. Emerging from local Neolithic groups around 400 B.C., the Dongson people were wet-rice cultivators who used water buffalo to prepare rice fields and lived in raised bamboo and thatch houses with built-in kitchens and vegetable gardens, features characteristic of lowland rice-cultivating villages throughout Southeast Asia today. The Dongson bronze drums, distributed widely in mainland and island Southeast Asia, indicated a supra-local ritual complex or trading network that linked mainland and island societies around 100 B.C. Scholars speculate that these Dongson drums were part of a ritual complex associated with chiefs with spiritual as well as political powers. Depictions of rice wine jars suggest that rice wine played a role in political rituals. Some scholars argue that the bronze in Southeast Asia was traded from the Shang state in China; others argue for local origins of bronze metallurgy in Southeast Asia. Iron was in use by A.D. 500 in Thailand, and likely elsewhere in the region as well.

Megalithic stone jars from the Plain of Jars, Lao PDR, 2002.

One of the most fascinating prehistoric sites in mainland Southeast Asia is the Plain of Jars in north central Laos, where immense stone jars, some as large as six feet in height and weighing over 10 tons, lay scattered across a limestone plateau. Considered part of an early megalithic culture, there are no other sites in the mainland with these features. These and other mysteries of the megalithic past will not soon be revealed since the area was bombed by the United States during the secret war on Laos in the 1960s and remains full of unexploded ordnance, making archaeological explorations difficult. Thailand has been able to develop a more extensive program of archaeological excavation. For countries like Burma, Cambodia, and Lao PDR, who must put food security as a higher priority for government spending, archaeology remains an expensive luxury. In addition, many sites such as Ban Chiang, Angkor Wat in Cambodia, and the Plain of Jars were either damaged by decades of war or were looted, their treasures sold to collectors and tourists.

HISTORICAL EVIDENCE

What was Southeast Asia like before the period of intense interaction with India and China? Historians and archaeologists speculate on the features of the communities before Indianization and Sinicization: cultivation of irrigated rice fields; domestication of ox and water buffalo; use of metals; skill in navigation; importance of women and maternal descent; worship of spirits (animism) and ancestors; and cosmological dualism opposing mountain with sea, coastal with upland, and male with female.[3]

Beginning with the reports of travelers from India and China, Southeast Asia began to be represented in a new and distinct manner—through written documents. The sketchy evidence from travelers in the early centuries A.D. often described the vibrant Southeast Asian societies as nothing but outposts of China or India in their national historical records. This image of the region as a cultural backwater was picked up and elaborated by colonial historians, and used to justify European intervention many centuries later.

Early historical scholarship on Southeast Asia was characterized by a search for origins, and for evidence of the various waves of "racial migrations" flowing north to south, first the Negrito pygmies followed by southern Mongoloids. The search for remnants of earlier waves of migration was also linked to language families. For example, historians speculate that Malayo-Polynesian and Mon-Khmer languages were spoken in the earliest historical kingdoms.[4]

Population expansion pushed groups farther south and into more marginal areas, no doubt with substantial intermarrying along the way. When the Tai[5] peoples moved down the river valleys into the mainland, they would likely have encountered Mon and Khmer groups with different ways of life.

Sinicization and Indianization

External influences on Southeast Asia at times and in certain places have been overwhelming. At other times and places the influence of external powers was minimal. Whenever Southeast Asian communities absorbed innovations from others, it was always done selectively and always redefined as local, whether it was a Portuguese dessert or a French baguette. Southeast Asian communities were great borrowers but what they borrowed was always grafted onto their own local traditions.

Chinese influence in Southeast Asia is most obvious in Vietnam. Chinese armies established a military outpost in 214 B.C. and invaded the northern region of Vietnam in 111 B.C., incorporating Nam Viet into the Han empire. They began the work of "civilizing" the peoples of Vietnam, introducing Confucian bureaucratic structures, a written form of Vietnamese based on Chinese characters, and Chinese styles of ritual and administration, including examinations. As the most Sinicized country in the region, Vietnam adapted principles of Chinese cuisine and today is the only country in Southeast Asia to rely primarily on chopsticks for all meals. The Vietnamese gained independence from China in A.D. 939, but Chinese influence in the country continued with periodic invasions.

Chinese settled in other parts of Southeast Asia as well; Chinese traders were settled around Jakarta before 1527, well before the Dutch renamed the city Batavia in 1618. They were trading in the Philippines by the eleventh century, leaving many Hokkien recipes and food practices to influence Tagalog cooking.[6]

Indianization refers to the influence of southern Indian traders and religious practitioners on Southeast Asia. They brought new religious traditions and texts—Hindu, Hindu-Buddhist, and Buddhist—new forms of dance, sculpture, and music, and new approaches to politics and statecraft that would transform local chiefs and chiefdoms into god-kings and kingdoms. These traders and Brahman priests were particularly knowledgeable about the rituals of royal courts. The local chiefs viewed Indian statecraft as a means of strengthening their own power. In particular, the idea of the god-king, or *devaraja*, helped legitimize local rulers, creating the Indianized kingdoms of mainland and island Southeast Asia. These kingdoms had no fixed boundaries but expanded and contracted in what was known as a *mandala* pattern, with a sacred center where the god-king resided, surrounded by tributary rulers.

The first known Indianized state was Funan, located in what is now Cambodia and southern Vietnam. Indian travelers reached the port towns of Southeast Asia by 200 B.C. or even earlier. Soon merchants brought new weapons, textiles, jewelry, and tools to the region. Roman coins and lamps, along with Iranian, Indian, and Chinese artifacts, were found at the site of the coastal trading port of Oc Eo in the delta of the Mekong River, evidence of the extensive trade network associated with Funan (A.D. 200–600).

Third-century Chinese reports describe walled towns and palaces in the coastal area. They referred to the sacred capitals of Indianized states as ceremonial centers where divine rulers administered agricultural lands. Reports describe displays of gold and silver jewelry, sarongs of brocade, raised wood houses, and large boats. Kings traveled with their concubines on elephants. The Mon kingdom of Tun San, known in Thailand as Dvaravati, was a dependency of Funan. By the sixth century, Funan lost control of most of its federation. Chen La, a successor state of Funan and an early Khmer kingdom, took over the Funan confederacy but soon retreated to the area of Tonle Sap in Cambodia.

Champa, begun in the second century A.D. in south and central Vietnam, was another maritime successor state to Funan. An Indianized state, it was later influenced by Islamic traders, and much of its population converted to Islam. Champa was gradually absorbed into Vietnam after its defeat by the Vietnamese in A.D. 1471. The remnants of Champa continued until the seventeenth century. The Chams spoke one of the few Austronesian languages on the mainland, and no doubt had close cultural ties to Malaysia and other Malayo-Polynesian speakers.[7]

Perhaps the best-known Indianized kingdom in Southeast Asia is the Khmer temple complex of Angkor Wat in Cambodia. Jayavarman II (802–850) established the famous Khmer kingdom of Angkor, which at its height held a million people. Khmer kings were *devarajas*, god-kings, worshipped in Hindu-style temple-palaces. Nearby Tonle Sap Lake, with its annual cycle of flooding and receding of rich alluvial lands, permitted the development of complex hydraulic systems and irrigation networks. The prosperity of Angkor was made possible by an abundance of fish from the Tonle Sap and the capacity of the land and population to produce two rice crops a year. Large-scale temple complexes reflected the gradual shift from worshipping the Hindu deities of Siva and Vishnu to venerating the Buddha. A hierarchical society based on slave labor produced surpluses for the royal centers in the form of rice, honey, sugar, spices, salt, and nonedible luxuries. Although Angkor and many of the Indianized states were hierarchical, often with Brahman priests supplying royal ritual services to *devaraja* rulers, Southeast Asia never fully adopted the Indian caste system. Only Bali retains some elements of the caste system.

A series of *devaraja* god-kings from the ninth to the fifteenth century ruled a far-flung Khmer empire that fell into gradual decline and was defeated by the Siamese kingdom of Ayuttaya in 1353 and again in 1430. Between these periods, Siamese and Cambodian rulers exchanged "people, ideas, texts, and institutions."[8] At the height of its power, Khmer palaces produced a refined cuisine, but by the fifteenth century, Khmer power eroded. Recipes associated with the Khmer palaces were modified in Ayuttaya and eventually re-exported into Cambodia.

During the same time period, to the west of the Khmer empire, the Mon people occupied the great Irrawaddy River delta. The Mon and Pyu kingdoms of Burma, also based on intensive wet-rice agriculture, were instrumental in bringing the Sri Lankan style of Theravada Buddhism to mainland Southeast Asia. To the north, the ninth-century kingdom of Pagan developed on fertile lands irrigated by the Irrawaddy River. With its 13,000 temples, Pagan dominated Burma from 1057 to 1287. While Pagan gained prestige and territory, the temple state never came into direct conflict with the Khmer empire. In 1057, when king Anawratha of Pagan conquered the Mon capital of Thaton, aspects of Mon culture, including cuisine, were integrated into Burmese culture.

Meanwhile, Tai speakers gradually moved southward from the seventh-century Nan Chao capital at Tali in the Yunnan province. Kublai Khan's conquest of Nan Chao in 1254 pushed larger numbers of Tai groups further south where they adopted the Theravada Buddhism of the Mon groups they encountered. Groups ancestral to present day Lao, Shan, and Thai drifted southward along the major river valleys—the Irrawaddy, Salween, Chao Phraya, and Mekong. They were in northern Burma by the seventh century, in northern Thailand by the ninth century, and in Laos by the eleventh century.

Sukhothai, considered the first independent Siamese kingdom, was a Khmer tributary state that claimed independence from Angkor around 1220. The best-known ruler, King Ramkhamhaeng (1279–1299), adopted Theravada Buddhism and identified himself as a *dharmaraja*, a righteous king following the rule of dharma or Buddhist law. In an important inscription, we find evidence of a Southeast Asian kingdom advertising its prosperity by reference to its food. An inscription from 1292 in Thai script reads, "In the water there is fish; in the fields there is rice," a phrase that is constantly invoked in discussions of Thai culture and cuisine.

The kingdom of Ayuttaya (1350–1767), a successor state to Sukhothai, harkened back to the Khmer style of the god-king or *devaraja*. Poised between the Burmese and Khmer empires, Ayuttayan kings fought against both kingdoms, defeating and being defeated by them both over the centuries. A new Siamese state, successor to Ayuttaya and developed near the present site of Bangkok on the Chao Phraya River, consolidated the current Chakri rulers as the longest-reigning dynasty in Southeast Asia. The British deposed Burmese King Thibaw in 1885, bringing an end to the Burmese monarchy and encouraging more Indian and Chinese traders into the country. Along with them, they brought their distinctive cuisines—cuisines that still dominate urban restaurants in the country to this day.

This brief historical sketch of the early history of mainland Southeast Asia illustrates the sweep and flow of successor kingdoms, the constant movement of populations, and the conversion to Theravada Buddhism of much of the mainland. The story reflects what has been called the "relaxed pattern of intra-regional relations" in Southeast Asia.[9] These relations brought the mainland kingdoms into contact with the islands, where Indianized states emerged as well. Indian influence stopped short of the Philippines; there Muslims and Christians vied for the souls of the local populations. The great ruin of Borubadur in Java is a reminder of the Hindu-Buddhist kingdoms that were established on the islands of Sumatra and Java. But the "relaxed pattern of intra-regional relations" in the region soon changed as Southeast Asia came into contact with a new set of players, attracted to a unique set of food products that shaped subsequent history in the region.

THE SPICE TRADE, ISLAMICIZATION, AND COLONIZATION

One of the most important parts of Southeast Asian food history is the search for and use of spices. Indianization, Sinicization, Islamicization, and colonialism are all implicated in the story of spices. At different times in the past, spices were among the most compact and profitable trade items; they were easy to store, ship, and sell in any number of ports for very high prices, and were used as a universal currency.[10]

Although historical sources can tell a great deal about the external pressures brought to bear on Southeast Asia through the search for spices, it is important to remember that although the region was a node in the trade between India and China, trade in spices did not start with the Portuguese traders' arrival in Southeast Asia; the existing trade in spices just became more visible to historians in the west.

Greeks, and later Romans, often made the yearlong voyage to India for spices. There is good evidence that the Greco-Egyptian dynasty of the Ptolemies made the trip regularly by 305–330 B.C., bringing back black pepper, cinnamon, cloves, and nutmeg, in addition to other luxuries. Spices helped to create the "first global cuisine" in Rome.[11] When Roman trade declined in the first centuries A.D., Arab traders took over the lucrative trade. After the rise of Islam, Arab merchants spread throughout the region, creating trading outposts from India to China, with Southeast Asia conveniently located in the middle of their trading routes. From India, Gujerati Muslim merchants married local women in Southeast Asia, and conversions to Islam spread out from the port cities.

While Muslim merchants continued to supply Europeans with spices, Venice dominated the spice trade by the ninth century, with spices such as cloves, mace, and nutmeg moving overland by the "silk route" of Central Asia, and from Arab merchants established in port cities along the coast of Malaysia and in the islands. Although Java was active in the spice trade, it did not produce spices for export. There was a great demand for spices in Europe. Spices were used to flavor monotonous winter diets and mask the taste of salted and pickled meats. Spices evoked paradise, displayed status, figured in cures, preserved food (and bodies), and generally "stirred the senses." Profit and fantasy inspired the European quest for these exotic items, which had been known in Europe since Greek and Roman times.

European Colonization

The Europeans colonized Southeast Asia for a variety of reasons—to obtain raw materials, to make use of cheap labor, to establish markets and settle excess population, to secure military advantage, and to increase national prestige.[12] The rationalization for imperial control often included the desire to civilize the locals and bring them the benefits of the western world, including Christianity. But colonial explorations were first and foremost for economic profit.

The European search for spices began in earnest in the late 1400s by the Portuguese, who were the first Europeans to claim empires in Southeast Asia and the last to leave their colonies in 1975. The Portuguese were excellent experienced seamen, aided by their development of innovative navigational instruments. Early in the fifteenth century, they set out on voyages of trade and discovery. Vasco de Gama reached India in 1498 with the intention of undercutting Arab spice traders and competing directly with Venetian spice traders. Portuguese traders set up small, fortified trading posts. They captured Malacca in 1511, the first European possession in the region. From this strategic spot, dominating the straits between Sumatra and the Malay Peninsula, they controlled trade in Southeast Asia for the next century. The Portuguese occupied a string of fortified ports in addition to Malacca on islands such as Flores, Timor, and Ambon in Indonesia. From these ports, they set out to locate the small volcanic islands of north and south Moluccas in eastern Indonesia—known as the Spice Islands, the sole source of cloves and nutmegs. Finding these small islands among the thousands of islands in the vast oceans of the Sunda Sea was no easy task.

By the seventeenth century, the Dutch and English entered the market, determined to control their own supply of spices, particularly black pepper, cloves, nutmeg, mace, and cinnamon. Their work was accomplished through trading companies: The English East India Company was chartered in 1600, and the Dutch East India Company (VOC) in 1602, the year the Dutch founded Batavia, now Jakarta. In 1641, the Dutch took the Moluccas from the Portuguese. By the mid-sixteenth century, annual exports of Moluccan cloves, nutmeg, and mace to Europe averaged 143,000 kilograms.[13] The Dutch effectively created a monopoly on spices, stamping out illicit trade and preventing any transplanting. As a result, the markup on cloves and nutmeg between purchase and final sale was close to 2,000%.[14] During the 1500s, the spice trade doubled in size, peaking by the end of the 1700s when other players entered the market and other products proved more profitable.

The Spanish had taken control of the Philippines by 1571. Over the next few centuries, most of the population converted to Catholicism, making the Philippines the most Catholic Christian country in the region. Following the Spanish-American war of 1898, the Spanish gave control of the Philippines to the Americans.

The trading ports established by the Dutch and the Portuguese had little direct effect on the lives of many Southeast Asian island communities—and even less direct impact on the mainland, which had fewer spices and stronger indigenous states. It was not until the nineteenth century that Europeans began to colonize the mainland, although earlier individual Europeans occasionally settled in the mainland for trade or missionary work.

By the early 1800s, European interest in Southeast Asia increased, motivated by a greater demand for raw materials such as tin, timber, sugar, and coffee, as well as markets for their new industrial goods. New innovations like steamships made contact easier and faster, and there was a growth in missionary zeal. As a result, by 1870, much of mainland Southeast Asia was under European control.

The British were the first to colonize the mainland, beginning with Burma, which they considered merely an extension of India. Singapore was founded in 1819 by a British colonial officer, and passed to the English East India Trading Company in 1824. The Burmese fought three Anglo-British wars, ceding territory each time, and became a British colony in 1886.

France's imperial history in Southeast Asia followed a different route. French Catholic priests in present day Vietnam became involved with helping political leaders modernize the country in the mid 1800s. Under pretext of religious persecution, Napoleon III invaded first Cochin China in the south, Annam in the middle, and finally in 1883 took Tonkin in the north, merging them into Indochina with the addition of Cambodia and Laos, making Vietnam virtually disappear. Earlier, in 1863, Cambodia had to accept French "protection" from Vietnam and Thailand, as had Laos in 1893. The French focused on Vietnam as the center of their civilizing mission, dismissing Lao and Cambodians as too lazy and child-like to benefit from French culture.

Thailand, known until 1939 as Siam, was the only country in Southeast Asia that was never colonized. It benefited from the fact that European powers competed directly with each other; the British competed with the Dutch in the islands and with France in the mainland. King Mongkut of Thailand (1851–1868) played a key role in keeping Siamese independence, but gave up territory in Laos, Cambodia, and Malaya (later to become Malaysia) to appease French and British imperial powers. Whereas Burma underestimated British power, Siam's monarchy and advisors appeared to understand both the threat of European colonialism and the advantages of European technology and scientific advances.[15]

The idea that Thailand remained independent because the country acted as a buffer for competing imperial powers has been challenged by Thai historians. Nevertheless, Siam never developed the anticolonial, antiwestern nationalism of the other countries in the mainland, and its transformation into a modern nation-state and a constitutional monarchy after a coup in 1932 was accomplished without wars of independence through a series of internal transformations.

The Effects of Colonialism

Assessing the long-term costs and benefits of colonial rule in mainland Southeast Asia is difficult because the full costs of colonialism are often hidden. In some countries, Europeans brought in European-style infrastructure, including centralized education and health services, but dismantled the indigenous systems of traditional medicine and temple schools in Theravada Buddhist countries. Colonialism forced the opening of more land for rice cultivation for export. The costs to indigenous subsistence patterns were great following the colonial emphasis on export cash crops such as rubber, rice, teak, and tea. Many small farmers lost their land to larger land owners better able to afford the costs of new technology required for plantation agriculture. Transformation to a wage economy began under colonial rule. As landless rural migrants swelled pluralistic cities such as Saigon, Rangoon, Singapore, and Bangkok, cities began to be seen as centers of culture, the home of urban elites who saw themselves as superior to the backward peasants in the countryside.

CULINARY COLONIALISM

Cuisines often carry with them the traces of their colonized pasts. Colonialism produced some of the practices and recipes adopted in Southeast Asia, but they had little effect on local attitudes towards food and taste preferences for most of the people in the region. Nevertheless, it is useful to identify specific taste transfers and new ingredients because they provide insights into how food cultures in the region change through time.

Before European colonization, Chinese and Arab traders brought island spices to the mainland, where they influenced many recipes, particularly Malaysian and Indonesian food dishes. Chinese influence on Southeast Asian cuisines is substantial. Chinese culinary traditions combine rice and accompanying "with rice" dishes. Noodles are likely Chinese imports, as are specific cooking techniques such as stir-frying. Elaborate Chinese banquets where courses are served sequentially and in a prescribed order are features of Southeast Asian urban life.

Indianization brought the coconut-milk style of Southeast Asian curries to Burma; curries once popular only in the courts are now considered to be characteristic of particular national cuisines. Indianization continued indirectly in the fifteenth century as Khmer cooks brought Indian-style coconut-based curries and boiled red and white sweets, used in Brahman-style rites of passage from Angkor Wat to Ayuttaya, and reintroduced them back into Khmer palace kitchens as Siamese armies ravaged parts of Cambodia.

By the 1600s, Portuguese and Spanish explorers began to bring New World plants to the region, including tomatoes, papaya, pineapple, corn, potato and sweet potato, and cassava. The greatest gift of the Columbian exchange to the food culture of Southeast Asia was the chile pepper from Central America, which rapidly replaced various indigenous peppers as a source of hot taste.

Among the traditional boiled desserts found in Southeast Asian markets from Burma to Malaysia are a series of sweet egg desserts also found in Kerala, South India. They are probably all derived from sixteenth-century Portuguese desserts. These Portuguese-style delicacies, still popular in Thai and Cambodian cuisine, are made from egg yolks cooked in boiling sugar syrup. Golden threads (in Thai, *kanom foi thong*) are made by letting the egg flow through a tiny hole in a container into boiling sugar syrup; *thong yip*, from dropping a spoonful of batter into the syrup; and *thong yod* from putting it into a small cup.

French colonialism affected the Lao, Cambodian, and Vietnamese food systems in many ways; French bread, pate, and salads clearly came from the colonial experience. Elegant Lao restaurants offer Luang Prabang salad made with mayonnaise, an example of the fusion of French salad traditions with the Lao practice of providing plates of raw or steamed vegetables and herbs to go with dipping sauces.

Luang Prabang Salad

The fusion of French and Lao salad traditions can be found all over the country, but this salad is considered best in Luang Prabang, the old royal capital of Laos.

1 head leaf lettuce

1/2 cup coriander leaves

1/2 cup watercress

1/4 cup mint leaves

2 chopped green onions

2 tomatoes, cut in slices

1/2 cucumber, finely sliced

2 large eggs, hard-boiled

2 tbsp chopped peanuts

2 tbsp oil

1/2 cup ground pork

6 cloves minced garlic

1/2 tsp salt

1 tbsp sugar

1/2 cup hot water

1/2 cup (scant) vinegar

Dressing

1 tbsp fish sauce

1 tbsp lime juice

1 tbsp minced ginger

2 chopped chiles

Assemble chopped washed greens in a bowl or platter. Cut hard-boiled eggs in slices after removing yolks. Mix the fish sauce, lime juice, ginger, chiles (to taste), and 1 teaspoon minced garlic together and set aside. Heat oil in wok; add remaining garlic and stir-fry until lightly browned. Add pork and stir-fry for 2 minutes; add water, salt, sugar, vinegar, and mashed egg yolks. Cook until well blended, and toss gently with greens. Immediately toss dressing over salad and decorate with chopped egg whites, tomatoes, cucumbers, and chopped peanuts.

The culinary effects of French colonialism are evident in the superb baguettes of the former Indochina, the Cambodian poulet au riz that can be served with rice or baguettes, and the use of mayonnaise and mustard in many dishes. Cambodian provincial beef salad resembles its Thai and Lao counterparts but adds sugar, red wine vinegar, and Dijon mustard. Cambodian dishes like lime-marinated beef salad, while similar to other Thai and Lao dishes, seem more refined, more like steak tartare than indigenous minced meat recipes such as Lao *laap* (see chapter 4).

The *banh mi* sandwiches (see recipe in chapter 4) combine French baguettes with Vietnamese-style sausages or barbequed meats, marinated vegetables, cucumbers, and coriander with mayonnaise and soy sauce. However, apart from freshly baked baguettes, the French had less impact on the Lao and Cambodian food system than on the Vietnamese.

Vietnamese and Cambodian cuisine also carries traces of the taste of imported French foods such as wine, coffee, and asparagus; the local elite may have come to truly appreciate French cuisine.[16] In order for Vietnamese and Cambodians to decolonize their tastes, do they have to learn not to like French foods, or to stop using mustard to flavor dishes? It is interesting to note that the French did not adopt Vietnamese or Cambodian taste preferences, although the British adopted the flavors of their former colonies, as did the Dutch. Processed foods like HP sauce, Worcestershire sauce, Peak Frean biscuits, and jams were marketed in the British colonies and even influenced local dipping sauces.

Nyonya Dipping Sauce

British colonialism also had effects through the import of processed sauces, including HP sauce and Worcestershire sauce. This Nyonya dipping sauce from Malaysia shows how British processed foods were incorporated into Southeast Asian meal staples.

4 tbsp Worcestershire sauce

3 tsp fresh lime or lemon juice

2 tsp soy sauce

2 tsp sugar

1–2 chiles to taste

Mix first four ingredients well in a small bowl. Add finely chopped chiles to taste.

Unlike Indonesian, Malaysian, and Vietnamese food, which bears the inscriptions of colonial taste preferences and technological innovations or impositions, the Thai food system has never been colonized. It has freely borrowed European food items and meal formats according to individual taste preferences and systems of cultural signification, within the limits set by state systems of marketing and food pricing. This includes the importation of individual western food items. Thailand has never had to reject any particular European food item, although some of the hybrid food items created never gained popularity. By the end of the 1800s, recipes for western-style almond cakes and other desserts such as ice cream were regularly published in the *Bangkok Gazette* in English. However, any European item that appealed to the Thai taste could easily be appropriated into newly emerging definitions of a national cuisine. As a result of never being directly colonized, the country never had to negotiate the decolonization of taste.

Unlike the relation between Britain and India, where Indian foods preceded Indian immigration to Britain and quickly became standard fare, European and North American interest in Thai food was unconnected to historical colonialism. Thai interest in western foods reflects the sustained Thai interest in trying new foods and flavors, without altering preferences for Thai tastes and meal formats. However, the opposition between "rice eaters" and "non-rice-eating others" remained; for all the curiosity of individuals about some items of western food, the food cultures of Southeast Asia never gave up rice for bread or potatoes.

INDEPENDENCE AND NATIONALISM

The processes of Indianization, Sinicization, Islamicization, and colonization are reminders that globalization is not a new process in Southeast Asia. The food systems of present day Southeast Asian countries reflect a long period of interaction with European foods, as discussed above. These important processes help explain contemporary conditions in the independent nations of Southeast Asia. In most of the countries of Southeast Asia, resistance movements existed long before official independence. For example, Saya San in Burma tried unsuccessfully to restore a Buddhist monarchy in the 1930s. When the Japanese drove the British from Burma, the Burmese found themselves mistreated by the Japanese. Burma gained independence in 1948. In 1962, a military coup in Burma created socialist rule, and by 1989 a new dictatorship reduced Burma to its current conditions, where protests are violently suppressed. Ho Chi Minh, educated in Vietnam and France, eventually formed the Indochinese Communist Party and returned to Vietnam in 1941, uniting Cambodian, Lao, and Vietnamese nationalists. The nationalist movements in Cambodia and Laos developed more fully after the Second World War. In 1941, Japanese forces attacked Southeast Asia to establish the Greater East Asia Co-Prosperity Sphere. But Japanese occupation of these areas did not bring about independence. Cambodia declared independence in 1953.

Ho Chi Minh founded the Viet Minh from the old Indochinese Communist Party to drive both the French Vichy government and the Japanese out of Vietnam. But the complexity of the divisions in Vietnam at the end of the Second World War set the stage for the Indochina Wars (1946–1954), resulting in the division between south and north Vietnam, and later, the Vietnam or American War (1964–1975). The American war in Vietnam killed 59,000 Americans; millions more Vietnamese were killed, wounded, and displaced. Both Cambodia and Laos became sideshows, deeply affected by the politics of the Vietnam War. Here too the American military propped up corrupt governments as long as they were anticommunist and bombed supply trails used by the Viet Minh. In the early 1960s, the Americans launched the "secret war in Laos," making Laos "the most heavily bombed country, per capita, in the history of warfare."[17] But the Pathet Lao, with the help of the Viet Minh, succeeded in setting up a communist government in Lao PDR in 1975. The secret war in Laos is less well known than the killing fields of Cambodia under the Khmer Rouge, a communist group that took over the government in 1975. From 1975–1978, the Khmer Rouge forced a communist revolution on the country, decimating nearly half of Cambodia's population of six million and forcing hundreds of thousands to flee as refugees, along with Lao and Vietnamese.

ASSOCIATION OF SOUTHEAST ASIAN NATIONS

The newly independent countries of Southeast Asia retained some conditions of dependency after independence—a dependency furthered through development projects.

Southeast Asia has been part of a number of trade and peace pacts, the most significant being the Association of Southeast Asian Nations (ASEAN), established in 1967. The member ASEAN countries (originally Indonesia, Malaysia, the Philippines, Singapore, Thailand; later, Brunei, Cambodia,

Lao PDR, and Vietnam, with Burma as observer status) agreed to close cooperation on projects of common interest such as the Mekong River project and regional trade. In addition, ASEAN cooperation and globalization brought increased international tourism to the region.

The financial collapse of 1997, starting with the Thai baht and influencing the economies of the region, changed the pattern of investment in restaurants and food enterprises in the region. However, recovery in the urban areas has been swift.

The tsunami of December 26, 2004, killed over 250,000 people in Southeast Asia, most in the Aceh province in northern Sumatra, many in Thailand, and some in Malaysia. In addition to the local and personal tragedies caused by the loss of life and destruction of property, the tsunami disrupted the flow of tourists to the region, particularly in the resort areas of Phuket in southern Thailand. Cyclone Nargis hit Burma in May 2008 leaving more than 134,000 people dead or missing and presumed dead. With many more wounded and left homeless, it is unlikely that Burma will open up even their restricted tourist market any time soon.

The ancient history of Southeast Asia helps explain the character of some of the typical meals one might encounter in visiting the region today. More recent history also explains why there are elegant Thai restaurants in North American cities where there are few Thai immigrants, why Lao cooks are found in the kitchens of those restaurants, and why noodle or *pho* shops are cropping up all over in North American and Australian suburbs. A brief answer is that Thailand has marketed its national cuisine better than most Southeast Asian countries, in spite of the fact that emigration from Thailand is very low and few Thais enter Europe or North America as refugees. Instead, the Thai government has encouraged the establishment of "authentic Thai restaurants" in North America, Australia, and Europe. Other than in Los Angeles, New York, and Chicago, Thai immigration to North America is not as high as the number of Thai restaurants would suggest. Demand is clearly coming from non-Thai, while Cambodian, Lao, Malaysian, and Vietnamese restaurants have tended to follow immigrant flows to the cities of North America and Europe.

NOTES

1. M. Laffan, "Another Andalusia: Images of Colonial Southeast Asia in Arabic Newspapers," *Journal of Asian Studies* 66, no. 3: 689–722.

2. Much of the information on the history has come from the excellent overview provided by R. Scupin in *Peoples and Cultures of Asia* (Upper Saddle River, NJ: Prentice Hall, 2006). See page 339 for prehistory.

3. D. Hall, *A History of South-East Asia* (New York: St. Martin's Press, 1970), p. 9.

4. R. Provencher, *Mainland Southeast Asia: An Anthropological Perspective* (Pacific Palisades: Goodyear Publishing Company, 1975), p. 19.

5. The term *Tai* refers to all speakers of related Tai languages, including the Lao and Shan, not just the present day Thai in Thailand.

6. Details of the influence of Chinese food in Indonesia and the Philippines, as well as in other parts of the world, can be found in D. Wu and S. Cheung's edited book, *The Globalization of Chinese Food* (Honolulu: University of Hawaii Press, 2002).

7. Scupin, *Peoples and Cultures*, p. 342.

8. D. Chandler, *A History of Cambodia* (Boulder, CO: Westview Press, 1983), p. 79.

9. O. Walters, *History, Culture, and Region in Southeast Asian Perspectives* (Singapore: Institute of Southeast Asian Studies, 1982), p. 28.

10. This section on the spice trade relies on the excellent historical research in Jack Turner's book, *Spice* (New York: Vintage Books, 2004).

11. Turner, *Spice*, p. 61, 67.

12. C. Tweedle and L. Kimball, *Introduction to the Peoples and Cultures of Asia* (Englewood Cliffs, NJ: Prentice Hall, 1985), p. 274.

13. Anthony Reid, *Southeast Asia in the Age of Commerce (1450–1680)*, vol. 1, *The Land below the Winds* (New Haven, CT: Yale University Press, 1988), p. 7.

14. Turner, *Spice*, p. 291.

15. Scupin, *Peoples and Cultures*, p. 347.

16. The writer of the *Elephant Walk Cookbook* writes that her father, educated in Paris but living in Cambodia, would only eat French food, p. 5.

17. Scupin, *Peoples and Cultures*, p. 355.

2

Major Foods and Ingredients

Southeast Asian culinary complexes include rice as the central source of calories and a dominant cultural symbol of feminine nurture, fish and fermented fish products, local fresh vegetables and herbs, and meat in variable amounts. Dairy foods are not traditional and have only recently been marketed among these largely lactose-intolerant populations.

RICE

Southeast Asia is primarily agricultural; rice, the dominant and preferred cereal crop, is also used for making noodles, rice flour, and rice wine. As the key staple, it is valued far beyond its nutritional value. In some parts of Southeast Asia, rice is not easy to grow; in areas where it flourishes, it still needs constant attention from humans to grow. Rice agriculture is more than a subsistence system; skilled technical practices become ritual acts and this ritual technology is work that must be accomplished for a good harvest. Rice has a soul that must be nurtured. The rituals associated with rice production are explored in chapter six.

Almost all cultivated varieties of rice belong to a single species, *Oryza sativa*, with about 120,000 varieties divided into two groups, tropical indica and temperate japonica.[1] The best-known Southeast Asian rice is the long-grained indica variety known as aromatic jasmine rice. High-yielding varieties of indica rice are widely grown in Thailand, Cambodia, and Vietnam, and exported to North America and elsewhere. Thailand is the largest exporter of rice at about eight million metric tons, followed by Vietnam at four million metric tons, an incredible accomplishment for a country whose agriculture was nearly destroyed by war.[2] In Thai, this rice might be referred to as *khaw chaw* (rice of the ruler), or *khaw suay* (beautiful rice). But while this is the rice that is most often exported, rice adapts to local conditions, and overwhelmingly it is the local regional variety that people prefer for their daily meals.

Irrigated wet-rice varieties are the most productive but rely on canals, terraces, and other labor-intensive techniques in order to flourish. Dry-rice varieties are grown in the uplands. Rain-fed lowland rice and deep-water rice are also characteristic of the region. Since the 1960s, high-yielding varieties of rice produced by the green revolution spread through Southeast Asia, increasing rice yields dramatically in most areas. However, the newer varieties, which required insecticides and fertilizers to produce these yields, damaged the delicate rice ecologies and encouraged the shift away from subsistence production. Today, most rice grown in the region comes from modern high-yielding varieties.

Rice for household consumption is always separated from seed rice to be used for the next season's planting and from rice that will be sold. Elder women select the best seeds of rice to be kept for seed.[3] The Shan refer to the rice for household consumption as *khaw tontrakun* (lineage rice).[4]

Transplanting rice in Banaue, Ifugao Province, Philippines, 2000. Courtesy of B. Lynne Milgram.

Rice is milled and polished in local rice mills or in rural households where foot-operated rice pounders remove husks from rice for the day's meals. Traditionally, rice is stored in sheaves or in threshed grains. In Southeast Asia, rice is not parboiled or treated in any other way.

Another key distinction is between glutinous and non-glutinous varieties of rice. Low in amylose and high in amylopectin, glutinous rice has very different cooking properties from non-glutinous rice; since it absorbs little water during cooking, it is usually steamed. The key marker of the collective identity of lowland Lao, northeastern and northern Thai, and many north Vietnamese groups is the use of glutinous or sticky rice as their daily staple. Glutinous rice is by far the preferred rice for the lowland Lao. More recent arrivals to Lao PDR such as the Yao and Hmong prefer to use non-glutinous rice. It is an understatement to say that the Lao appreciate the qualities of glutinous rice; like their north Vietnamese neighbors, they believe that glutinous rice is more nutritious and more aromatic than any other kind of rice. In Vietnam, contests were held to perfect glutinous rice steaming skills for young girls and men.[5] Users are very conscious of the aromatic and cooking qualities of glutinous rice, as well as its keeping quality. This is equally true of families with adequate rice and families who must buy rice because their own fields have not produced enough or who have no access to rice fields.

Rice surveys in Lao PDR have found over 3,200 rice varieties in the country, 85% of them glutinous.[6] Glutinous rice is generally hardier and survives draught, salinity, and floods better than its non-glutinous relatives. Most glutinous rice is consumed close to its place of production. It is eaten by hand and is extremely difficult to eat with fork and spoon. The technique is easily learned: Form a ball by hand with a thumb-size indentation, scoop up some sauce or side dish, and enjoy. And no rice tastes better than rice grown at home. While Lao and Vietnamese who use glutinous rice as their daily staple celebrate the taste of their local rice varieties, a European visitor in 1877 did not like the "stickiness" of glutinous rice, referring to it as that "ghastly rice of Laotians."[7]

While Lao make distinctions between people who eat glutinous rice and those who eat non-glutinous rice, in fact, the distinction is somewhat arbitrary and is breaking down rapidly. Ordinary or non-glutinous rice can become glutinous, and glutinous rice can become ordinary rice, as the glutinous character of the rice endosperm is reversible. Lao, Shan, and many Vietnamese groups have selected for glutinous characteristics that increase with domestication.[8] However, many groups grow both kinds of rice; although the Shan eat glutinous rice for everyday meals, they use non-glutinous rice for medicine and gift exchanges.[9] Elsewhere, glutinous rice is grown for making desserts, rice flour, and rice wine. Unpolished black and purple varieties are particularly popular for making special desserts.

Because of government policies to reduce swidden upland agriculture and to increase production of cash crops, Lao farmers with access to irrigated fields have been encouraged to produce non-glutinous rice for sale. The government of Lao PDR, for example, provides Thai glutinous and non-glutinous seed varieties to various communities and groups to encourage the growing of rice for export. The few new varieties of glutinous and non-glutinous rice grown in irrigated fields in the central region of Lao PDR since 1993 require fertilizers, mechanical threshers, and hand tractors in order to make a profit.[10] The small amounts of glutinous rice exported for use by overseas Southeast Asians comes from northeastern Thailand, and Lao consumers find Thai rice less flavorful than the rice they remember from home villages. Thus, glutinous rice may not be the primary marker of Lao ethnic identity for much longer.

CORN AND OTHER STAPLE FOODS

Corn was probably brought to Southeast Asia from Central America by the Portuguese or the Spanish, starting from the 1500s, as part of the Columbian Exchange. It is grown in many upland areas as a dependable, filling staple, and in the lowlands as animal feed. Corn on the cob is sold on the streets in Southeast Asian cities, grilled and dipped in a chile, salt, and sugar mixture. Corn is also used in a variety of iced and non-iced desserts such as tapioca and corn pudding with coconut cream, popular in Vietnam and Thailand.[11] Cornstarch has been integrated into noodle-making recipes, and baby corn is a popular ingredient in stir-fry dishes. Millet and sorghum were grown in the past in some upland communities.

Roots, tubers, and corn make up starchy bulky foods available to more food insecure marginal communities. In some parts of Southeast Asia, cassava, a New World crop, is collected wild as an emergency food; in other areas, it is planted in upland fields as a dry season crop; in Thailand, it is grown for animal fodder. But wherever root crops are grown in Southeast Asia, they are freely given up for the more prestigious rice: "Rice advances across Southeast Asia as if it were addictive."[12] But root crops are never entirely abandoned. In the forests of Lao PDR, wild yams, cassava, and taro are collected by women who know where to find them and how to process them to remove poisons, if necessary, by soaking, cooking, and drying the roots. Lao elders report that many young people have no idea how to find or process wild cassava, although they recall eating it mixed with rice when rice supplies were low. In other parts of the world, knowledge of how to process toxic tubers has already been lost, resulting in deaths from cyanide poisoning.[13] Once harvested, cassava tubers are very perishable and hard to store. Cassava tubers have a high carbohydrate content and are a good source of potassium, iron, magnesium, vitamin C, and other vitamins.

SOY PRODUCTS

Soy sauce has been used in China for over 2,500 years and is used in most Southeast Asian communities. Traditionally, soy sauce is made from the liquid produced when soybeans are boiled with wheat and fermented; however, synthetic versions of soy sauce are often sold commercially. Fermented soybean paste adds a sour or astringent taste to Shan, Lao, and northern Vietnamese dishes, and is available bottled in North America. Soybean cakes or tofu are common in the region, and were introduced by Chinese traders. Tofu is made from the liquid from mashed soybeans mixed with a coagulant and water and pressed into cakes; it is easily integrated into a wide variety of vegetarian dishes. Other soy products such as tempeh were developed by the Javanese centuries ago, and Indonesian cuisine provides the tastiest recipes using these products. The process begins by removing the skins from the soybeans, boiling them, mixing them with a special yeast culture, and fermenting the mixture into cakes of tempeh that can be battered, deep fried, and made into a variety of dishes. Dishes from tofu, tempeh, and eggs are integral to Indonesian and Malaysian cuisine.

FISH AND SEAFOOD

It is impossible to overstate the importance of fish and fermented fish products to Southeast Asian diets. Freshwater fish, sea fish, and shellfish are the major source of protein for most meals. The Mekong River has supplied people from Lao PDR, Thailand, Cambodia, and Vietnam with a steady supply of river fish for centuries. The favorite, the giant Mekong catfish, whose properties have reached mythical proportions, is near extinction. Snakehead, catfish, and mackerel are popular fish in the region. In Cambodia, the Tonle Sap (Great Lake) supplies a large variety of freshwater fish for much of the population especially during the rainy season. In late November, when the waters of Tonle Sap crest and begin to run backwards, freshwater fish are scooped up in quantity. Cambodians process this fish in a variety of ways, including making a preserved fermented fish product, *prahok*, in order to make full use of the seasonal surplus all year. Cambodian cuisine uses *prahok* as an ingredient and features various forms of freshwater fish and freshwater lobster and clams. The products are also dried and salted.

The Vietnamese, Malay, and Indonesians also enjoy a long sea coastline that gives them access to an abundance of fish plus lobster, crab, squid, and shrimp. Many rural Southeast Asians raise fish in ponds near their homes and rice fields. People seek out fresh fish in rivers, streams, or ponds late in the day to eat for the evening meal. Fish and other seafood are widely available in the open markets. Small sun-dried and salted fish are popular additions to meals throughout the year. Fish are most plentiful in the rice fields after the rainy season (October to December). Lakeside, riverside, and seaside restaurants feature regional specialties of fried, smoked, grilled, or salted fish. Fish is included in roll-ups and in stir-fries, simmered in soups, or grilled on open charcoal fires. In Thailand, some dishes such as the ubiquitous *pat Thai* (Thai fried noodles) or *somtam* (papaya salad) are unimaginable without the addition of small dried shrimp or ground shrimp. Today, raw fish dishes are discouraged as public health

Dried fish for sale in Vang Vieng market, Lao PDR.

officials consider them unhealthy. In the past, fish heads were prepared as a special dish for royalty. Now fish head, especially cheeks, is a common dish in Chinese restaurants.

Shrimp Simmered in Caramel Sauce

This simple, elegant Vietnamese dish uses a French technique of making a caramel sauce to enhance flavor and color.

1 lb shrimp, peeled and deveined

1 tbsp fish sauce

1/2 tsp black pepper

2 tbsp caramel sauce (see below)

1 small yellow onion

green onion for garnish

Combine shrimp, fish sauce, caramel sauce, chopped yellow onion, and pepper in a saucepan. Bring to a boil and simmer at medium heat for around 10 minutes until the sauce is dark brown in color. Transfer the shrimp to a shallow bowl and garnish with green onion.

    Caramel Sauce: Melt 1 cup of sugar in 3/4 cup of water. After the sugar caramelizes, remove from heat and continue stirring until black in color. Let cool and pour into a jar. Keep in a cupboard until needed. (Some cooks add fish sauce directly to the caramel sauce.)

FERMENTED FISH PRODUCTS

Accompanying most rice meals across Southeast Asia is a sauce or paste made from fermented fish or shellfish. The fish are salted, dried, pounded, and packed with toasted rice and rice husk in jars for a month or more. Fish products that are fermented become "cooked" and are no longer considered raw. Fish sauce (in Thai, *nam plaa*) is a crucial ingredient in most Thai, Lao, Khmer, and Vietnamese dishes. These flavorful sauces perk up rice meals even for the very poor, who may not have many side dishes to eat with rice. The Vietnamese version is called *nuoc mam* and is a basic ingredient and condiment present at all meals. A fermented shrimp paste, *mam ruoc*, is also used for flavoring dishes. Anchovies are the preferred product to use in Vietnam, while Cambodians use catfish or snakehead fish. These fermented products provide the distinctive taste in most Southeast Asian cuisines.

In its thicker form, fermented fish is served as a dish with rice; this is called *padek* in Lao and *prahok* in Khmer. Rice husks along with salt break

Padek (fermented fish) for sale in a market in Palse, southern Laos, 1999. Courtesy of S. Bush.

down the fish. Special ceramic jars that absorb the odor are used for this purpose. The strong-smelling product is not appealing to many westerners who have little tolerance for fermented, fishy foods, but overseas Southeast Asians speak longingly of the taste of local versions recalled nostalgically from their homeland.

For the Burman, the prized accompanying dish of fermented anchovies is called *ngapi*. This product can be made from different types of dried fish. After drying the fish or shrimp in the sun, it is mashed up with salt and packed into jars. The resultant material is pungent and a highly prized condiment to eat with rice. The Thai call a similar product of fermented salted shrimp *kapi* and the product is usually mixed with chile peppers. It is also used in Malay and Indonesian dishes. The English colonists of the Malay Straits Settlements adopted the Malay word, *balachan*, for this dish made from small fish or shrimp, along with salt and spices. These fermented fish products can be served alone as condiments or made into more complex sauces. Most often, fish sauce is mixed with chile peppers. The Thai term *nam prik* refers to a fish sauce mixed with ground roasted chiles and other local ingredients according to the region of the country to produce *nam prik plaa pon* (with the addition of ground dried fish), *nam prik plaa raa* (with the addition of fermented fish), *nam prik kapi* (with the addition of shrimp paste), or *nam prik ong* (with the addition of ground pork and tomatoes). The same pattern exists for *jeaw*, the Lao version of a hot chile sauce.

Commercial fish sauce is widely available throughout Southeast Asia and in overseas Asian markets. It is not made by scooping off the water from fermented fish such as *padek* or *prahok,* but rather from sea fish with salt and preservatives added so that it can be made faster and transported throughout the region and around the world.

The World Health Organization (WHO) warns against using home-processed fish in either fermented or raw dishes because of possible liver flukes. Local health professionals argue that it would be better to promote improved processing techniques rather than ban the use of a product that is so basic to Southeast Asian cooking.[14] The Vietnamese are particularly careful to use only the highest grade fish sauces in their cooking.

VEGETABLES

Greens, vegetables, and aromatic herbs are available from household gardens and local markets, and they are particularly valued for their freshness and texture. Recent development projects on home gardens in rural areas of Southeast Asia have dramatically increased the amount of fresh vegetables available to households. Families participating in these pilot projects consumed three times more vegetables than they sold. However, households need land, labor, and seeds to benefit from these initiatives.

A common vegetable, water spinach, also known as swamp cabbage or water morning glory, is popular all through the region, where it is used in soups and in quick stir-fries. Elsewhere in the world it is considered a noxious weed. Probably of southern Chinese origin, it spreads anywhere there is water and has many close wild relatives in Vietnam, Malaysia, Thailand, and Cambodia. In Burma, it is even used to relieve opium poisoning. This vegetable, as well as some other common greens, is probably available free or at very low cost to most rural households.

Fried Morning Glory/Water Spinach

This easy-to-prepare stir-fry dish to accompany rice is widely available and has many regional variations, such as topping it with a fried egg.

1 tbsp oil
1 slice finely chopped ginger

1 clove finely chopped garlic

1–2 chile peppers, finely chopped

1 bunch washed and chopped water spinach/morning glory

splash of soy sauce or Maggi sauce

Heat the oil and add chopped ginger, garlic, and chiles. Stir-fry over high heat and add greens. Season with Maggi sauce or soy sauce, and add water if pan gets too hot. Serve over rice.

Other vegetables are served in soups; stir-fried with onions, garlic, meat, or fish; or served raw or lightly steamed with fermented fish products as dipping sauces. They are key ingredients in dry and wet curries. Eggplants come in a wide variety of forms, from long green or purple plants used for grilling or stir-fries to tiny bitter pea-like plants flavoring Thai and Lao curries. Other popular vegetables include banana blossoms, bitter melon, lotus, bok choy, rapini, napa cabbage, sweet potato, green onions or scallions, Chinese chives, bean sprouts (from soy and mung beans), and a wide variety of local greens.

Experimental vegetable plots in Lao PDR, 2002.

River weed (*khai*), as it is known in northern Lao PDR, is a variety of green algae (Chlorophyceae) collected from the fast-flowing rivers of northern Laos and Thailand. It is harvested in winter, from November to January, and from stagnant water in the rainy season. Families collect the bright green algae, which looks like fine seaweed, from rocks on the sides of rivers. Related to Spirogyra, it is rich in vitamin A; one variety is used to make agar-agar for desserts, sour salads in the Philippines, and *khai pen* in Lao PDR. To make *khai pen*, the algae is spread in the sun to dry and processed by pressing dried tomatoes, garlic, chiles, sesame seeds, and salt into the dried sheets. The sheets are held together with tamarind paste. It can also be cut into strips and used as a flavoring in vegetable dishes or fried rice, or grilled and served as a snack with drinks.[15]

Squashes can be stuffed with coconut custard as a dessert, in addition to their use in stir-fry dishes, curries, and soups. New vegetables are easily adapted into traditional recipes. For example, jicama was brought to the Philippines from the New World by the Spanish in the seventeenth century; from there it spread throughout Southeast Asia, perhaps because it is so useful for salads such as the one below.

Woman selling vegetables in a neighborhood market in Hanoi, Vietnam, 2008.

Jicama and Pineapple Salad

This fruit and vegetable salad is called *rojak*, or "mixed" in Malay, and is considered a Nyonya dish with Javanese roots. Many different versions are available from street vendors in Malaysia and Indonesia.

Select about 4 cups of salad ingredients cut into matchsticks or wedges:

1 small jicama

1 unripe mango

1 cucumber

half a pineapple

1 tart apple (experiment with other fruit and vegetables)

Dressing

2 tbsp brown sugar

2 tbsp soy sauce

2 tbsp tamarind water (from tamarind paste)

1 tsp shrimp paste

1–3 chopped chiles

chopped peanuts for garnish

Grind or blend dressing ingredients together. Mix well into salad mixture and let stand for half an hour before serving. Garnish with chopped peanuts.

Wild foods from the forest, including wild ferns, bamboo shoots, and roots, provide food in times of emergency food shortages or regular expected hunger seasons, and they add unique tastes—often bitter or sour—as well as nutrients not always available in cultivated plants.[16] As fewer people gather wild foods, the knowledge about locating and processing these foods is being lost; at the same time, the environment where they can be found is changing due to the destruction of forests.

Forest foods such as mushrooms, aromatic herbs, and water clover are popular ingredients in salads, pickles, and stir-fry dishes. Mushrooms come in a wide variety of forms and are available fresh or dried in both cultivated and wild forms, particularly in the rainy season. Rural villagers and upland groups use local wild vegetables and herbs in their daily meals; they may also sell the surplus on roadsides for cash. With declining forests and fewer swidden farms, wild forest specialties such as edible ferns rarely make it into urban markets. Travelers from Lao towns and cities stop by the side of the road when they see people with baskets of vegetables, hoping to find a rare taste treat to buy. The Lao in particular still remember the taste of wild foods, and thus seek them out when they travel.

Elders, both male and female, generally know where to locate wild plant products if they still live in localities where they were first taught to locate and process these items. However, people who have been relocated may not know where to obtain wild foods, particularly medicinal herbs, and also may not know how to process them to remove toxins. Correct processing and prescribing requires specialized knowledge.

MEAT

Meat is rarely the central focus of a Southeast Asian meal, and many dishes make use of only a small quantity of pork, beef, or chicken in a recipe. The taste of meat is not featured except in grilled meats. When meat is available, the whole animal is used, and often guts and brains are considered delicacies and are just as expensive as muscle meat, particularly in Chinese dishes. In the past, dishes like pig entrails in blood were a common breakfast dish. Lao dishes such as *laap* contain intestines, as do many other soups and specialties found in rural areas. Chicken, goose, and duck feet were used to flavor soups and stews. However, this does not mean that poor households prefer the taste of chicken feet to chicken legs, for example.

Wild animal meat such as wild boar, barking deer, and civet cat are both rural specialties and elite food. Soft shell turtle was a rare delicacy in the

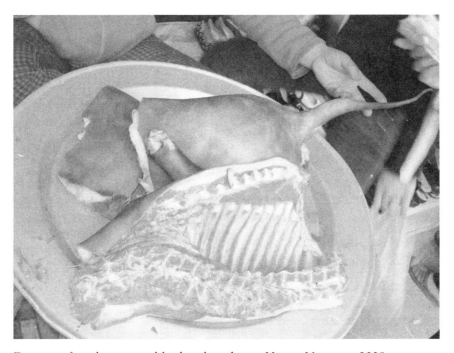

Dog meat for sale in a neighborhood market in Hanoi, Vietnam, 2008.

past, but is no longer available or desired. Wild-animal markets, mostly illegal, supply wild food from endangered species to specialty restaurants in some urban centers. Dog is considered a delicacy among Hmong and some Vietnamese groups.

Sausages are popular as well, particularly in Vietnamese and Cambodian meals. Northern Thai make a fermented pork sausage called *naem* with a distinctive sour taste.

In many countries in the region, local Chinese families controlled the raising and selling of pigs. Since the Chinese also played important roles in the development of urban restaurants, pork is one of the most important meats in restaurant dishes in non-Muslim Southeast Asia. In the past, pig fat was very popular for frying; however, more healthy vegetable oils are now preferred.

Squirrels, snakes, frogs, and wild birds also supply protein in rural and upland communities, although there is clear preference for chicken, pork, duck, or beef should cash be available to purchase meat. Insects, including crickets and ants, have protein, poly-unsaturated fatty acids, and minerals, and are sold deep fried in rural and urban markets. Upland communities carry out sophisticated seasonal hunting with nets and traps, and have an intricate system of sharing hunted meat among kin.

Domestic animals in poor rural communities do not fare well without regular vaccinations, although development projects often attempt to improve domestic livestock and poultry. Most projects fail unless external aid projects are able to provide extension support in the form of vaccinations and access to veterinarian services.

SEASONINGS

Southeast Asian cuisine has been described as a balance of hot, sour, salty, and sweet. These flavors are accomplished by blends of spices and herbs, all locally available and highly valued. It was spices that first drew Arab and European traders to the region. And spices still form an integral part of Southeast Asian dishes. Dried spices such as cloves, nutmeg, and cinnamon play a larger role in flavoring Malaysian and Indonesian dishes. Mainland cuisines make greater use of fresh aromatic herbs. Spices and herbs are used in the form of leaves, flowers, stems, seeds, or roots, and add flavor, texture, and aroma to dishes.

Throughout Southeast Asia there is a clear continuity between medicinal and culinary use of herbs and other forest products. Ginger, coriander root, turmeric, pennywort, and aromatic woods, for example, play important roles in both medicinal and culinary systems. As with wild vegetables, the elders know what wild plants have medicinal qualities, and how herbs can be combined for best results in both medicinal and culinary uses.

Salt iodization at Boten, northern Lao PDR, 2002.

Salt is critically important to human diets. Many parts of Southeast Asia rely on salt to make fish sauce and fermented fish pastes to supply salty fishy flavor. Inland groups such as the Shan prefer to use salt to flavor dishes and kill bacteria. Boiled salt was an important trade item in northern and northeastern Thailand and Lao PDR. With the high rates of goiter in the upland area of Lao PDR and Vietnam, UNICEF and other UN agencies began programs to encourage the use of iodized salt. The salt evaporation industry at Boten, near the border of China and Lao PDR, added a chloride to the evaporated salt to make iodized salt for local use. In many mainland markets, the price of iodized salt was much higher than non-iodized salt, and since salt was also provided to domestic animals, villagers were unlikely to purchase small expensive packages of iodized salt.

Salt Mixtures

Salt is highly valued and used as a condiment with rice and whatever else is available in the poorest households in rural Southeast Asia. This Burmese version mixes sesame seeds and salt.

3 tbsp sesame seeds to 1 tsp salt

Heat seeds and salt, stirring constantly in a small, dry pan until seeds brown (3–5 minutes). Grind by hand or machine and serve as a condiment with rice dishes.

The Thai-Lao version mixes chiles and sugar with the salt to create a dip for raw vegetables or fruit.

Pound together 1 tsp roasted chile powder with 2 tbsp salt and 3 tbsp sugar.

At dawn in any Southeast Asian village, the pounding sounds of mortar and pestle announce the processing of the ingredients for flavor pastes to be used that day. Flavor pastes are used in stir-fry dishes, soups, and curries. Items are added to a stone, wooden, or ceramic mortar one at a time and pounded, starting with the hardest and driest ingredients and ending with softer wetter ingredients. Since the use of flavor pastes reflects locally available spices and herbs, as well as personal and traditional taste preferences, it is difficult to generalize about recipes for flavor pastes. To capture the range of ingredients used in Southeast Asia, one begins with chile peppers, since they are found in the most basic flavor pastes of garlic, salt, shallots, and chiles. Other ingredients most likely to be found in Southeast Asian kitchens are listed in alphabetical order by their common English name after a discussion of chile peppers.

It is hard to imagine Southeast Asian food without the heat of fresh and dried chile peppers. But chiles first entered the region only in the sixteenth century, brought from the New World by Portuguese traders as part of the Columbian Exchange. Chile peppers were introduced to Africa and Asia and rapidly integrated into Southeast Asian cuisines as a substitute for varieties of long peppers (pippali); they probably also replaced black pepper common in Euro-American food in some recipes. Black pepper, dried berries from India and Indonesia, was sometimes harvested while still green; white pepper is picked when ripe, soaked in salt, and dried. It is used in barbequed chicken (gai yang).

Chile is the Aztec word for pepper and was in use 6,000 years ago in Ecuador. Roasting or cooking intensifies the hotness of peppers, while soaking reduces their fiery heat. The irritant in chile peppers is called capsaicin, and has a number of anti-infective properties. The heat is concentrated in the inner membranes and the seeds of the peppers. Large green or yellow chiles are milder and often grilled; the small red and green "bird's eye" chiles common in Thai food are the hottest. Dried packages of chiles are commonly found in Asian grocery stores. Other popular seasonings include:

Basil (including Asian basil, lemon basil, and holy basil) is a variety of sweet basil, and widely used in salads and stir-fry dishes throughout the region.

Betel seeds can be chewed with betel pepper leaf smeared with red lime and other leaves and seeds. The betel quid acts as a stimulant and increases saliva production.

Cardamom, a relative of ginger, is widely used in Cambodia and Vietnam.

Cinnamon or cassia bark is usually sold in sticks or ground to a powder and used in Malay and Indonesian dishes.

Cloves are small black flower buds of a plant found in the Spice Islands, the Moluccas, and have medicinal properties. They are common in Malay and Indonesian food.

Coriander leaves, stems, seeds, and roots are all used. The seeds are usually ground, while the leaves and stems are popular in a wide range of dishes. The roots are important in Thai-Lao cooking. A long-leafed version with a serrated edge is used in Vietnamese and Cambodian soups and eaten raw in northeastern Thai-Lao dishes.

Curry powder is a commercial product developed originally by the British to imitate the dried spice mixtures (masala) used in Indian cooking. Locally made curry powders are used in Burmese and Malaysian cooking.

Galangal is a relative of ginger used in Thai, Lao, Khmer, Vietnamese, and Indonesian cooking (where it is known as *laos*). It is used in soups and curries.

Garlic is used in most regional cuisines as part of the flavor paste.

Ginger is a tuber grown throughout Southeast Asia. Ginger has medicinal properties and is often used to make a healing hot drink, ginger tea.

Lemongrass is an herb native to Malaysia. The tough stalks provide a popular flavor in soups and are ground to make Thai, Lao, Khmer, Vietnamese, Malay, and Indonesian flavor pastes.

Mace is the membrane on the nutmeg, usually sold in the form of a powder.

Mint leaves are used fresh in Lao and Vietnamese salads and in meat dishes.

Nutmeg comes from the Spice Islands, the Moluccas. It is grated into many Malay and Indonesian dishes.

Pandanus leaves add flavor to steamed dishes and are used as wrappers and plates.

Sakhan is an aromatic wood used in Luang Prabang, Lao PDR to provide a distinctive bitter taste to stews.

Sesame seeds from the sesame plant are often dry roasted and used for snacks and desserts.

Shallots are a variety of small red onion used in flavor pastes and stir-fried dishes.

Star anise is important in Vietnamese cooking, particularly for making *pho* soup.

Tamarind is often used in the form of paste made from the tamarind pod dissolved in water. It gives a sour taste to soups and stews. Pods are obtained from wild and cultivated trees. Both leaves and flowers are eaten. Tamarind plants have a long history of medicinal use as astringents, laxatives, and to lower blood pressure.

Turmeric root is related to ginger, and gives a yellow color to dishes. It is common in
Burma, Malaysia, and Indonesia, and also has medicinal uses as an antiseptic.

Wild lime and wild lime leaves are used to flavor stews and soups.

Often herbs are grown in small kitchen gardens, bamboo baskets, or in B-52
bomb shells scavenged from war-ravaged areas of Vietnam, Cambodia, and
Lao PDR.[17]

FRUIT

Southeast Asia is a fruit lover's utopia. It has been written, "Borneo is
the center of tropical fruit diversity. Most fruits that are even partially
cultivated have close cousins within the Bornean forest."[18] Fruit is used in
salads and pickles but is most often consumed as snacks or desserts.

Coconuts are used in a variety of ways; Malays dry roast fresh coconut
until it is brown, grind it, and add it to cooked dishes. Elsewhere in the
mainland countries, the white meat found in mature coconuts is grated
fresh and used to make thick or thin coconut milk used in curries. Young
coconuts contain refreshing coconut water that can be consumed from
the green coconuts. This product is not used in curries. Coconut cream
is used most in Malaysian dishes and in palace dishes derived from the
royal courts of Cambodia and Thailand. It is rarely used in Chinese dishes.
Many Southeast Asian desserts combine coconut milk with palm sugar.
Palm sugar, the sap of the sugar palm, has a rich creamy flavor that is hard
to replicate with brown sugar or cane sugar.

Preparing fresh fruit for sale, Bangkok, 2005.

Bananas, native to the region, come in many varieties, and are eaten as snacks and used unripe and ripe in a variety of desserts. Some varieties are believed to have medicinal properties, particularly the banana flower, which is often used in soups. Citrus fruits include the grapefruit-like pomelos, oranges, lemons, kumquats, and a variety of wild and cultivated limes. Jackfruit is served fresh and in iced desserts; the roots have been used to cure diarrhea. Mangoes are used in salads and pickles when green and unripe, and when ripe, they are used in a variety of desserts. Perhaps the best known to travelers to Southeast Asia is mangoes and sticky rice.

Mangoes and Sticky Rice

When mangoes are ripe, they are sold on the street with packets of sweet glutinous rice flavored with coconut milk.

4 sliced mangoes

3 cups sticky rice

2 cups canned coconut milk

1/2 cup brown sugar

1 tsp salt

mint for garnish

Soak rice overnight and steam until it is translucent (about 20 minutes). Heat coconut milk, sugar, and salt, stirring until dissolved. Pour 1 cup coconut milk over the glutinous rice and mix well. Let sit for half an hour. Serve a square or mound of sticky rice with slices of mango. Pass remaining coconut milk to serve on top of rice and mangoes.

Durian is a fruit people are seldom neutral about; they either love it or hate its strong smell and distinctive taste. The Columbian Exchange brought fruits such as papaya and pineapple to Southeast Asia. Papaya is now one of the most popular fruit in the region; it is eaten unripe in salads and in sour soups, and ripe as a fruit snack, often with lime juice. Pineapple is one fruit that is often used in savory dishes including soups.

NOTES

1. Francesca Bray, *The Rice Economies: Technology and Development in Asian Societies* (Berkeley: University of California Press, 1986), p. 16.

2. USDA trade figures for 2003.

3. From the Ifugao in the Philippines to the various Tai groups in the main-land, women are considered the best judges of seed rice, perhaps because they are intimately aware of their cooking properties. For details, see the papers in Roy Hamilton, ed., *The Art of Rice* (Los Angeles: UCLA Fowler Museum of Cultural History, 2003).

4. Ing-Britt Trankell, "Cooking, Care, and Domestication: A Culinary Ethnography of the Tai Yong, Northern Thailand," *Uppsala Studies in Cultural Anthropology* 21 (1995): 115.

5. Nguyen Xuan Hien, *Glutinous-Rice-Eating Tradition in Vietnam and Else-where* (Bangkok: White Lotus, 2001), p. 57.

6. A. Rao, et al., *Collection of Rice Germplasm in the Lao PDR between 1995 and 2000* (Vientiane, Lao PDR: National Rice Research Program [NAFRI], 2001).

7. Nguyen, *Glutinous Rice Eating*, p. 64.

8. Nguyen, *Glutinous Rice Eating*, pp. 20, 26.

9. Trankell, "Cooking, Care, and Domestication," p. 116.

10. J. M. Schiller, et al., "Glutinous Rice Varieties of Laos: Their Improve-ment, Cultivation, Processing, and Consumption," in R. Duffy, ed., *Specialty Rices of the World* (Rome: FAO, 1998), p. 226.

11. Most Southeast Asian cookbooks have recipes for this dessert. A particu-larly good one can be found in Jeffrey Alford and Naomi Duguid's *Hot Sour Salty Sweet* (Toronto: Random House Canada, 2000), p. 294.

12. Richard O'Connor, "Agricultural Change and Ethnic Succession in Southeast Asian States: A Case for Regional Anthropology," *Journal of Asian Studies* 54, no. 4 (1995): 986.

13. Paula Cardosa, et al., "Processing of Cassava Roots to Remove Cyano-gens," *Journal of Food Composition and Analysis* 18, no. 5 (2005): 451–460.

14. See Leedom Leffert's discussion in "Sticky Rice, Fermented Fish, and the Course of a Kingdom: The Politics of Food in Northeast Thailand," *Asian Studies Review* 29 (2005): 253.

15. I discuss river weed and *khai pen* in more detail in my article, "From Hun-ger Foods to Heritage Foods: Challenges to Food Localization in Lao PDR," in *Slow Food/Fast Food: The Cultural Economy of the Global Food System*, ed. R. Wilk (Lanham, MD: Altamira Press, 2006). Alford and Duguid (2000) also refer to recipes using river weed on page 165 of *Hot Sour Salty Sweet*.

16. Information about wild plants comes from Christiane Jacquat's use-ful book, *Plants from the Markets of Thailand* (Bangkok: DK Books, 1990). Jutta Krahn's PhD dissertation includes a detailed case study of wild plant use in Sekong province, southern Laos. See Jutta Krahn, "The Dynamics of Dietary Change of Transitional Food Systems in Tropical Forest Areas of Southeast Asia: The Con-temporary and Traditional Food System of the Katu in the Sekong Province, Lao PDR" (dissertation, Rheinische Friedrich-Wildhelms Univeritaet, 2005). The loss of wild plants also affects the use of natural dyes used to dye silk and cotton cloth.

17. Krahn, "The Dynamics of Dietary Change," p. 62.

18. Anna Tsing, *Friction* (Princeton: Princeton University Press, 2005), p. 178.

3

Cooking

Cooking is both art and science; as in other parts of the world, not everyone in Southeast Asia cooks with the same level of skill or the same aesthetic sense. Nevertheless, even the poorest households produce tasty meals using simple techniques like boiling, steaming, and grilling. This chapter discusses the division of labor in the kitchen, kitchens and their equipment, and the steps in acquiring, processing, and preparing food. In Southeast Asia, cooking means to prepare food for consumption, not just to apply heat. Thus fermenting, sun drying, and preparing raw dishes are discussed here as part of the cooking process.

Southeast Asian meals require the freshest possible ingredients, and lots of time (and skill) to process and prepare them, but cooking times are short and the cooking techniques are easily learned. In addition to taste, smell, appearance, and texture are important to Southeast Asian cooks. The harmony of tastes and textures, and the balance of hot/spicy, sour, salty, and sweet, is the basis of the complexity of Southeast Asian cuisines. Thai food is reputed to be the hottest cuisine in the region, but not all Thai dishes are hot. The Lao and the Shan of Burma and Thailand prefer more bitter and sour tastes, and Cambodian food, while similar to Thai in many ways, has less chile heat. Malay cooking makes greater use of coconuts than Lao cooking, for example. But these are all variations on the same Southeast Asian culinary themes.[1]

Southeast Asian cuisines are not vegetarian, although meat flavors do not dominate except for grilled meats. Nevertheless, meat is highly valued.

The poorest households only consume meat dishes on special occasions. Theravada Buddhists are not vegetarian; however, new vegetarian fasting traditions are emerging in urban centers. In many recipes, vegetarians are advised to substitute soy sauce for fish sauce, omit shrimp paste, and use tofu instead of meat. However, since meat and fish in small amounts are valued parts of peasant cooking throughout Southeast Asia, vegetarians in the region may find that local restaurants simply remove the meat from dishes, an inadequate response for fastidious western vegetarians who might expect that fish sauce, shrimp paste, or oyster sauce would not be used in the flavor pastes of "vegetarian" curries, for example. That is rarely the case in Southeast Asian cooking.

WHO COOKS?

The division of labor for cooking is not strict; both men and women may be recognized as skilled cooks in homes and restaurants. Generally, men learn to cook from men, and women, from women. Grilling of meats is most often done by men. Some ethnic groups, such as the Khmu of Lao PDR and other groups dependent on hunting, entrust cooking all meat

Author's daughter at 18 months, learning to cook Thai food with toy utensils and real cleaver, 1974.

dishes to men. However, everyday food preparation and rice cooking is usually done by women and young girls. Helpers, including children, first learn how to cut vegetables for different dishes. A Burmese cookbook author recalls that her mother made the best chicken curry and her father the best beef curry.[2] In many communities, including the Shan and Khmu, men are more likely to cook foods for ritual occasions. Men generally cook outside the house, away from the hearth. Among the Shan, men grate the coconut.[3]

Southeast Asian meals are best prepared collectively. The lone cook has little opportunity to prepare multiple dishes to go with rice without help cutting vegetables or processing flavor pastes. Activities like making desserts are often done communally with friends and relatives helping at all stages of the process.

Not all Southeast Asian communities recognize differences in cooking skills. While Thai villagers can easily identify the best cooks in the community, Lao villagers laughed at such a question and mixed dishes made by several women together in one serving dish, regardless of differences in seasoning and choice of vegetables. Similarly, towns such as Luang Namtha in northern Lao PDR have almost no cooked food for sale in markets or restaurants. Perhaps communities need to be food secure before they can differentiate skill levels in cooking. Many Lao households may only have tasted dishes made by family members and neighbors. As the opportunities for travel and trade expand, comparisons and experimentation will likely increase.

Cooking techniques in Southeast Asian households are not learned through cookbooks, although Thai cookbooks authored by celebrities sell well in a market that is fascinated with elite cooks and royal meals. Thailand's beloved monarch, King Bhumibol Adulyadej, contributes to the popular interest in all things royal by permitting books to be published by the Royal Projects Foundation about the food served at royal banquets and the favorite dishes of the royal family. In addition to the books published by the foundation, Princess Sirindhorn hand wrote and tested a series of recipes published in *Krua Sra Pathum* (Sra Pathum's Palace Kitchen) including Boston baked beans and Boston brown bread, His Majesty's favorites from his childhood. Professional chefs may read cookbooks to learn what is new in Hong Kong or Singapore, but chefs expect that books will not reveal all secrets about a dish and will not contain a complete listing of all ingredients.

Chefs such as Malaysia's Chef Wan Ismail are gaining a global audience through their cookbooks in English and their television cooking shows. Known as the food ambassador of Malaysia, Chef Wan cooks a variety of

Asian and western dishes. His work, as well as that of many other Southeast Asian cookbook authors, reinforces the point that a chef does not need be of a particular ethnicity to cook the foods of that ethnicity. In North American cities, many Lao chefs cook in Thai restaurants. Even in Chinese restaurants in Bangkok, Lao or Isaan chefs from northeastern Thailand may do the cooking, rather than Chinese or Sino-Chinese.[4]

In the decades since World War II, it was common for urban middle-class and elite households in Malaysia, Thailand, and Vietnam to have servants, including cooks; children from these households may never have learned to cook, and may be forced to learn from cookbooks as adults. Male students from Thailand and Vietnam studying overseas had to learn to cook or give up the tastes of home. They too seek out cookbooks in their local languages. In Thailand, the idea of recording favorite family recipes has a long history. Since the late 1800s, cremation volumes—small books given away at funerals—often included cooking instructions and favorite recipes of the deceased.[5] These volumes provide a glimpse into cooking practices of elite urban Thai families.

KITCHENS AND THEIR CONTENTS

Kitchens are ritually important places in traditional Southeast Asian houses, and their location in the house is related to both cosmology and to the sexual division of labor. That is, houses and the kitchens within them are not simply physical structures, but replicate cultural values; they are microcosms of the universe.[6] Most houses in rural Southeast Asia (with the exception of Vietnam) are raised well above ground to catch the breezes, with kitchens integrated into the back or veranda of the house. The hearth and cooking area may be lower than the platform where elders sleep and where religious activities take place. Some communities have separate cooking houses to keep the heat, smoke, and smells away from the living space; kitchens within the house may be considered the domain of women, while the outside kitchens, primarily grills, are the domain of men. A porous clay pot for water often sits on the veranda for visitors and family. The slaughter and preparation of chickens and ducks would be done outside the kitchen or in the market (or at the supermarket in cities).

What are kitchens like, and what is in them? For the rural poor, kitchens are sparse and may contain only an open fire or a closed ceramic or cement bucketlike stove (often coated with metal from flattened tins), a mortar and pestle, cutting board, bamboo steamer, cleaver, wok, spatula, ladle, coconut grater, and baskets for storing rice, vegetables, and spices. The space is always clean and uncluttered, as the equipment is usually hung vertically on hooks. Women and children work squatting on the floor or on low stools. One of the most interesting kitchen items is the coconut grater, formerly in every rural kitchen but now found mainly in antique stores. They are small wooden stools, carved like rabbits with "grater teeth." Coconut-shell implements are rapidly being replaced by plastic in communities with markets and a cash economy. Dishes may be limited to a few enamel plates or bowls. Food may also be served in cucumbers, coconuts, and pineapples, or wrapped in banana or pandanus leaves.[7]

Southeast Asian kitchens may also have very specialized equipment for making desserts and snack foods. Only the older generation of women is likely to know how to make these special foods. Today, the special snack foods and desserts once associated with the royal courts in Thailand and Cambodia are more likely to be purchased from food vendors who have acquired the traditional equipment and the skills to make these specialties.

Urban Southeast Asian households have kitchens as modern and elaborate as Euro-American kitchens, with electric refrigerators, stoves, rice cookers, microwave ovens, and a wide range of specialized appliances from local, Japanese, and European suppliers. But these modern urban homes may also have a simple village-style kitchen behind the house with a charcoal stove, grill, and mortar and pestle for preparing traditional dishes.

Most Southeast Asian kitchens will have bottles of fish sauce, soy sauce, and seasoning sauce close at hand, as well as containers of iodized salt, sugar, and MSG (monosodium glutamate). MSG can be found in almost all Southeast Asian kitchens, regardless of income. This flavor enhancer borrowed from the Chinese and Japanese in the last few decades is available everywhere, without concerns about whether it makes some people sick. Even the poorest kitchens have MSG, even when they do not have oil or iodized salt.

FOOD ACQUISITION

Many households and communities in Southeast Asia are self-sufficient in food. But these households are usually in the marginalized corners of the uplands. The number of people in Southeast Asia who can feed themselves entirely outside of the cash economy is diminishing rapidly. Food comes from wet-rice fields, dry upland fields, household gardens, hunting, fishing, and gathering wild vegetables and fruits, often from forests.

Food acquisition in rural areas can be as simple as reaching out the back door to grab a handful of edible greens such as watercress or morning glory leaves. In small rural villages throughout Southeast Asia, direct patron-client relations distribute and redistribute food within the community.

One household may regularly provide another with fresh vegetables, in return for emergency supplies of rice in the hungry season or for help with special occasions such as weddings or funerals. These food-based debts are never fully repaid, for to do so would be to end reciprocal relations basic to community survival.

In cities, towns, and even large villages, women shop every day for fresh produce, meat, and fish, patronizing the vendor who supplies the freshest produce for the best prices—someone who might provide short-term credit if necessary. Food acquisition in urban Southeast Asia offers the choice to shop in open markets offering produce, meat, fish, and bulk or packaged dry staples from all over the region or in air-conditioned supermarkets carrying the same range of staples, carefully packaged, along with food products from all over the world.

FOOD PROCESSING AND PREPARATION

Food processing takes place in rural and urban households as well as in small and large-scale commercial enterprises. Fermented fish products, the most important processed foods in mainland Southeast Asia, are processed in rural households but are more likely to be purchased already prepared at the market in towns and cities where modern neighbors might not appreciate the smell emitting from jars of fermenting fish.

Other items can be fermented as well, including bamboo shoots and bean curd. Often the water used for washing or initial cooking of rice is used in the fermenting process. Sun drying is another useful food processing technique in communities without refrigeration. Vegetables can be sun dried, as well as beef, water buffalo, and leftover glutinous rice. Vegetables may also be salted or pickled in vinegar to form the basis for sour salads or side dishes.

Preparation techniques for vegetables include washing and cutting diagonally into bite-size or matchstick pieces. Finely chopped garlic and ginger, for example, must be prepared ahead, as many dishes are assembled at the last minute.

Many ingredients such as chiles, garlic, and shallots are dry roasted before cooking to intensify their flavors. Roasted glutinous rice powder optionally ground with lemongrass or wild lime leaves adds texture and taste to northern Thai and Lao dishes; dry-roasted sesame seeds mixed with salt flavors Burmese dishes; even black pepper and salt can be dry roasted and ground, with or without dried chiles.

Roasted rice powder is an important element in Lao and Cambodian cooking. It is made by dry-roasting glutinous rice in a dry pan until brown and fragrant. Cool and grind to a powder. It can be stored in the refrigerator for several weeks.

The preparation of flavor pastes is an early morning task that links cuisines across the region. The skill of making these flavor pastes separates ordinary cooks from extraordinary cooks. Throughout Southeast Asia, regions, communities, and even households vary in the mixtures used to marinate meat and fish, and to make wet curries. Ingredients—dry and hard first—are ground by hand or grinder to a smooth paste or left as a grainier mixture, as preferred by Indonesians.

The technique may have come from southern India, by way of the royal courts of Indianized Southeast Asia. The recipes reflect taste preferences, locally available spices and herbs, and trade routes. Burma has the most direct Indian borrowings, adding turmeric to the mixture of chiles, garlic, ginger, and onions.[8] Another version traveled from India, by way of Java, into the Khmer courts, and from there into the royal kitchens of Ayuttaya, Thailand, adding cardamom and tamarind to replace the turmeric. Cambodia and Thailand add lemongrass and galangal to the mixture; Malaysia makes more use of wild lime leaves; Vietnam adds more star anise. Malaysian and Indonesian dishes make greater use of the spices that first drew the Europeans to the area—cinnamon (or cassia), cloves, and nutmeg. Dry roasting of ingredients before cooking releases the taste and aroma of the flavor pastes.

PRINCIPLE METHODS OF COOKING

Cooking Rice

Most Southeast Asian meals are based around rice; while "with rice" dishes may be room temperature, rice and soup are served hot. Cooking methods are related to techniques in China and India, and overlap substantially with cooking terms used in English, such as steaming, boiling, grilling, and stir-frying.

Cooking is connected to religious obligations in Buddhist and Muslim communities. In the Theravada Buddhist countries of Burma and Thailand, and to a lesser extent in Lao PDR and Cambodia, rural and urban households cook rice at dawn for distribution to monks on their early morning alms rounds. This means that boiled or steamed rice is available for family breakfasts. The best dishes the family can afford are prepared for the monks early in the morning; later family and neighbors can enjoy the rest of the dishes for their breakfast meal. Some families only prepare special food for the monks on the days when religious services are held in the community temples of Burma, Thailand, Lao PDR, and Cambodia.

This practice is in decline in many cities, where modern lives preclude this daily offering. In Muslim communities in Java, for example, ritual obligations involving food are more likely to occur at the end of the day in the form of the slametan feast. When staples like rice are cooked influences meal times and has implications for how leftovers are handled and who has access to them. When rice is cooked in the early morning, for example, leftover rice may be available for children's school lunches.

Cooking rice demonstrates a woman's skills. In Vietnam, there were contests to see who cooked the best glutinous rice. Girls of 10 should be able to cook rice properly. There are many methods for cooking rice. First, wash the rice to remove husk fragments; stir with your hands until the water rinses clear, and drain. Add cold water to a depth of about one inch above the rice. Bring to a boil, then simmer for about 10 minutes until most water is absorbed. Cover tightly and reduce the heat to very low for another 10 minutes. Remove from heat and let sit until ready to serve. Or use an electric rice cooker, a foolproof method that leaves the cook free to work on other dishes. Glutinous rice must be soaked in water for several hours or overnight before steaming in a conical shaped bamboo (Lao) or wooden (Shan) steamer. The cooked rice is then turned out, patted with a paddle or wooden spoon to remove lumps, and packed in rice baskets until ready to eat. The Lao bamboo steamers and the pots that they fit into are available from Asian grocery stores wherever Lao immigrants live. The idea of eating unpolished brown rice is not appealing to most Southeast Asians, who value the whitest, most polished rice they can afford. Brown rice was served in the past to prisoners and soldiers. Now health stores are introducing brown rice as a healthy option, on analogy with North American health foods and macrobiotic diets.

The taste qualities of glutinous and non-glutinous rice are very different, and they fit into meal patterns differently. In some Khmu communities in southern Lao PDR, for example, villagers grow and consume more non-glutinous rice not because they prefer the taste, but because it can be made into a filling soup to which other foods can be added. The shift indicates a shortage of rice not a change in taste preferences. Upland peoples in Lao PDR, Vietnam, and Cambodia often had only 1–4 months of rice during the war years. They stretch rice with roots and tubers such as cassava.[9]

Soups, of course, are boiled, and vary from the simplest flavored water of many Burmese and Lao soups to the elaborate French-inspired broths of Vietnamese dishes. Some Thai, Malay, and Cambodian soups are made more complex by the use of flavor pastes. All over Southeast Asia, rice soups and noodles soups make appealing breakfasts and snacks.

Stir-Frying

Stir-frying over high heat in a small amount of oil is considered a Chinese technique adopted by Southeast Asian cooks. Since the cooking technique is now so widespread, its point of origin is of less importance than understanding variations in heat intensity and fuel source. In Southeast Asia, stir-frying is considered the last step in preparing a dish to go with rice. Vegetables are washed and dried, cut evenly, and cooked quickly over high heat with small amounts of meat, fish, and seasonings. Vegetable oils are commonly used now; pig fat is unacceptable for religious reasons in Muslim communities, and is in decline for health reasons elsewhere.

Cambodian Pork and Eggplant Stir-Fry

This simple eggplant stir-fry dish could be made with other vegetables as well.

3 eggplants

2 tbsp oil

5 garlic cloves, coarsely chopped

1/2 lb ground pork

2 tbsp fish sauce

1 tbsp sugar

small bunch of garlic chive blossoms, cut in 2-inch lengths

ground black pepper

Prick eggplant and grill or roast for 40 minutes until soft. When cool, peel and mash the flesh. Stir-fry garlic in oil until golden, and add pork. Add fish sauce, sugar, and pepper. Add eggplant and chives, stir-frying until well mixed, and serve with rice.

Grilling

Grilling food over wood or charcoal has a long tradition in Southeast Asia, from the satay sticks sold along the roadsides of Malaysia, Java, Thailand, and Lao PDR, to the elaborately spiced grilled fish of Cambodia. Grilled vegetables also add texture to many different recipes. When the cooking is done over an open fire as in Lao PDR, Cambodia, Burma, and many upland groups, grilling is particularly easily accomplished. There wrapped food (*mok*) is roasted on hot embers. Children in Lao PDR grill frogs, fish, and insects over small fires.

A common sight in villages and cities of the region are vendors with tiny bucket charcoal stoves grilling small skewers of meat or vegetables,

Woman in Vientiane prepares grilled chicken in her outdoor kitchen, 2002.

much like kabobs of Persian cooking. The best satay in the region were
once grilled at Singapore's Satay Club, a collection of outdoor food vendors who used to grill handfuls of satay skewers over blazing fires.[10] Street
vendors use large grills for their products, and of course, commercial gas
barbeques are popular in middle-class urban households. Every barbeque
cookbook has recipes for satay, and any of the sauces in this book would
be suitable for dipping, in addition to the famous peanut sauce common
in Malaysia and Indonesia.

Flavor pastes can be used as marinades for fish or meat dishes. Fish and
chicken pieces are easily turned on a grill when they are wedged between
strips of split bamboo.

Gai Yang, Lao-Style BBQ Chicken

This Lao favorite traveled through northeast Thailand into the specialty shops of
Bangkok. Once a marker of Thai-Lao identity, it is now one of the most popular
dishes in Thai restaurants, an example of the appropriation of a devalued ethnic
food.

1 chicken, split open (or use legs and thighs)

Marinade

1 stalk sliced lemongrass

3 tbsp coriander roots, minced

pinch salt

1 tbsp fish sauce

2 tsp white pepper

5 cloves garlic

moisten paste with coconut milk if necessary[11]

Grind marinade ingredients in a small food processor. Rub into the chicken pieces and marinate at least 3 hours or overnight in the refrigerator. Grill until bottom side is brown; turn over and grill until juices run clear. Serve with steamed glutinous rice and papaya salad.

Baking

Professional baking skills are not widely distributed in Southeast Asian populations, although there are pockets in Indonesia where women with special skills in Dutch baking prepare cakes and cookies in the Dutch style. In the former French Indochina, breads and pastries from French recipes are seldom made in homes since the necessary ovens are absent, and wheat flour is expensive to import from temperate countries. Bread and pastries can be purchased from professional bakers who sell their products on the streets of Phnom Penh, Hanoi, and Vientiane. The wonderful baguettes found in Vietnam, Lao PDR, and Cambodia are not available in neighboring Thailand, Burma, or Malaysia. A legacy of French colonialism, baguettes have made their way into Indochinese cuisine at breakfast and in the form of baguette sandwiches that blend French and Vietnamese food items (see recipe for *banh mi* in the next chapter).

Palace Cooking

The palace kitchens of the Indianized royal courts in Thailand and Cambodia, the imperial the courts of Hue, and the Muslim sultanates of Malaysia and Indonesia always produced more elaborate cooking. Food prepared for the king or the rajah had to be tasted first to ensure the highest quality and to avoid food poisoning. In the 1800s, western cooks were hired to teach western-style dishes to palace cooks. Culinary skills for women were particularly highly valued. The service of royal wives and concubines provided the extra effort necessary to make elaborate meals with theatrical garnishes; time-consuming carving of fruit and vegetables displayed royal power. Even a carved flower made from a green onion, a chile pepper, or a radish could turn a simple stir-fry into a dish fit for a king. The Thai royal tradition in palace food has been made public in a number of cookbooks, complete with instructions for vegetable carving and for making time-consuming, difficult elements like egg nets. These delicate nets were spread over special royal dishes. The recipe book of the chef who cooked for the former Lao royal family in Luang Prabang has been translated into English and provides a glimpse into meals that resemble everyday Lao meals, except that they feature the best fish and meat.[12] Not much is known about the food served at the royal court at Mandalay. In general, Southeast Asia is not a region that differentiates a high cuisine from a low cuisine. Rather, the same techniques are used in both palace and village cooking, with the former distinguished by the use of more rare, expensive ingredients, elaborate garnishes, and elegant serving dishes.

Shortcuts

This chapter has shown that in Southeast Asia, food preparation and processing is much more complex than cooking, which may be accomplished very quickly in stir-fried or grilled dishes. But it would be a mistake to assume that Southeast Asian cooks never take shortcuts. Like busy women everywhere, not every day can be devoted to food preparation. A recent book on Bangkok's foodways describes plastic-bag housewives, who pick up bags of wonderful side dishes on the way home from work from street vendors.[13] Once home, electric rice cookers make monitoring the timing for cooked rice a thing of the past. Electric grinders and blenders shave hours from complex food-processing tasks such as making flavor pastes.

Supermarkets in the cities of Southeast Asia provide precut ingredients to simplify cooking tasks in households no longer employing cooks. Many elements of a Southeast Asian meal can be prepared ahead in quantities and kept in jars or frozen for later use. For example, fried onions and garlic can be prepared in quantity and stored in jars; curry pastes can be ground in amounts sufficient for several meals; caramel sauce for Vietnamese cooking and ground toasted rice for Thai-Lao dishes can all be prepared and stored for later use; and canned coconut milk and rice paper make meal preparation easier for urban cooks and displaced Southeast Asians in North America. Canned bamboo shoots are acceptable substitutes in American kitchens.

The popularity of Thai food overseas has been reinforced by the availability and promotion of semiprepared Thai food in food kits (also for sale in major airports in Southeast Asia). Outside of Southeast Asia, flavor pastes have recently become available in powdered, canned, and frozen forms, lessening the burden for new Southeast Asian immigrants to Australia, Europe, and North America who want to make the dishes they remember from home. To release the flavors, one fries the paste in oil or heats it in coconut milk, as in the following recipe.

Fish in Red Curry Sauce

A fish dish like this is served for special occasions in Thailand. The availability of packaged red curry paste makes this dish easier to prepare than grinding the spices by hand.

1 whole fish (about 2 lbs, red snapper is good)

3 tbsp oil

2 tbsp red curry paste

1 tbsp chopped ginger

2 cups coconut milk

1/4 cup fish sauce

3 tbsp sugar

5 thinly sliced wild lime limes

Clean fish, leaving the head and tail on. Make several slashes on each side. Stir-fry curry paste in oil for 1 minute. Add coconut milk, ginger, fish sauce, sugar, and fish. Cover and cook 20 minutes, turning the fish once. Garnish with finely sliced wild lime leaves.

As more Southeast Asians settle in North America and Europe, fresh herbs, vegetables, and other regional specialties such as lemongrass, wild lime leaves, tamarind paste, and galangal have become available in Asian food markets at reasonable prices. This makes it easier for people who have recently come to appreciate the taste of Southeast Asian food to reproduce some dishes in kitchens far from Southeast Asia. In addition, culinary tourism to Southeast Asia and international cooking schools have encouraged the production of special iconic or marker dishes such as *pat Thai* or satay that come to substitute for the great diversity of local dishes in the region. Nationalism is a key component in the promotion of these cooking schools as well as government efforts to promote Thai restaurants abroad. These iconic dishes are discussed in chapter 4.

NOTES

1. Cookbooks that focus attention on food across national borders in Southeast Asia, such as Jeffrey Alford and Naomi Duguid's *Hot Sour Salty Sweet* (Toronto: Random House Canada, 2000) and Rosemary Brissendon's *Southeast Asian Food* (Singapore: Periplus Editions, 2007), have particularly valuable discussions of these comparative cooking principles.

2. Susan Chan, *Flavors of Burma: Myanmar: Cuisine and Culture from the Land of the Golden Pagodas* (New York: Hippocrene Books, 2003), p. 86.

3. Ing-Britt Trankell, "Cooking, Care, and Domestication: A Culinary Epigraph of the Tai Yong, Northern Thailand," *Uppsala Studies in Cultural Anthropology* 21 (1995): 117. She also noted that kathoey or male transvestites may be inclined to specialize in the provision of cooked food for entertainment, p. 104.

4. This may be because chefs are not considered to be of high status in Thailand.

5. I discuss the content of these cremation volumes in Thailand in my article, "From Marco Polo to McDonald's: Thai Cuisine in Transition," *Food and Foodways* 5, no. 2 (1992): 177–193.

6. David Thompson claims that Thai kitchens should face north. *Thai Food* (Berkeley, CA: Ten Speed Press, 2002), p. 6.

7. Leaves and food vessels are used in the poorest households out of necessity because no other utensils are available; among the wealthy elite, use of these products emulates the palace cuisine with their elaborate decorative use of leaves in addition to vegetable carving techniques.

8. Chan, *Flavors of Burma*, p. 59.

9. Jutta Krahn, "The Dynamics of Dietary Change of Transitional Food Systems in Tropical Forest Areas of Southeast Asia: The Contemporary and Traditional Food System of the Katu in the Sekong Province, Lao PDR" (dissertation, Rheinische Friedrich-Wildhelms Univeritaet, 2005), p. 58.

10. Alexandra Greeley, *Asian Grills* (New York: Doubleday, 1993), p. 107.

11. White peppercorn, coriander root, and garlic is a very basic and ancient combination in Thai-Lao cooking and has its origin as a medicinal combination.

12. Phia Sing, *Traditional Recipes of Laos* (London: Prospect Books, 1981), p. 198.

13. Gisele Yasmeen, *Bangkok's Foodscape: Public Eating, Gender Relations, and Urban Change* (Bangkok: White Lotus, 2006).

4

Typical Meals

The noodles found in markets in Southeast Asia provide a clue for addressing the commonalities in food items, recipes, and meals in the region. In an area of such incredible ethnic and ecological diversity—an area identified as the crossroads of the world for two millennia, where traders and whole populations have moved regularly—what would constitute evidence for typical meals? Even national cuisines in Europe claim regional diversity in culinary traditions.

Cookbooks and cookbook categories may not give a clear picture of how typical meals are assembled in Southeast Asia. Instead, they sometimes impose western categories such as appetizers, soup courses, and casseroles to very different meal systems. In addition there are great differences in the meals of poor marginalized peoples and the new middle class in cities like Manila, Jakarta, Penang, Singapore, and Bangkok. It is also difficult to identify typical Southeast Asian dishes and meals as opposed to Chinese dishes in urban contexts where Chinese have contributed so much to the food cultures in the region. Generally, Southeast Asian meals share with Chinese meals the importance of rice with meat, vegetable, and fish side dishes, while Southeast Asian meals place more importance on spicy dipping sauces, raw and lightly steamed vegetable dishes, pickles, and soups made with tamarind and coconut milk.

Taste is in the mouth of the beholder; local and western chefs claim that Cambodian dishes are less sweet than Malaysian, and less salty than

Vietnamese; that Thai dishes are hotter than Vietnamese and Burmese; that Cambodian cuisine makes less of a distinction between fruits and vegetables than Malay; that Lao dishes are more bitter and sour than Thai dishes; that Vietnamese dishes are lighter than Chinese; or that groups like the Shan and the black Tai prefer salt to fish sauce. As always, generalizations are matched with local and personal exceptions to the rules.

This chapter approaches typical meals by describing some common meal elements, meal format, and the timing of meals (meal cycles). Typical meals are presented as "variations on a common theme," with particular attention to contrasts such as rural-urban and palace-village. Finally, iconic meals and dishes carry special meaning as markers of ethnic or national identity.

MEAL MANNERS

Urban meals are served on tables with chairs or benches, but rural meals may be enjoyed while sitting on woven floor mats or at low bamboo or wood tables. Muslim households make careful accommodation for hand and face washing before meals for religious reasons; the Lao provide places for hand washing for more pragmatic reasons, since they, like most Burmese, eat with their hands. Glutinous-rice eaters use small balls of sticky rice as scoops for side dishes. As with other groups in the region, leaves and greens can also be used as wrappers to carry food to mouth. Across the region, forks and spoons are the easiest, most efficient way to handle rice

Faculty at the National University of Laos share lunch, 2005.

and side dishes, with chopsticks used primarily in Vietnam, or for noodles and Chinese dishes.

Ideally, every side dish should have its own serving spoon, and every common bowl of soup, its ladle. In poor households, utensils may not be sufficient, so that individual forks, chopsticks, or soupspoons may move from mouth to common bowl, a situation known to be unhygienic and potentially a route for the transmission of hepatitis. On the other hand, eating with washed hands and using serving spoons, as in Lao, Burmese, or Malay villages, is relatively hygienic.

It is common for people to offer the best pieces from a side dish to others at the table. A choice piece of fish or meat, for example, might be picked up with chopsticks or fork and placed on the plate of a favored relative or guest. Wives might select a few special tidbits for their husbands. But the direction of giving is not predictable. A person of high status might well decide to give choice pieces to underlings as a mark of a good patron who looks after his or her clients. It is particularly rude to refuse such food offerings.

When there are several side dishes, it is appropriate to take a small amount from one side dish at a time, rather than pile a selection of all side dishes on a plate of rice at once. The latter is considered both rude and foolish, as mixing the side dishes makes it difficult to appreciate the taste contrasts and personalize mouthfuls. Dry and wet condiments are placed directly on rice or on the side of the plate.

PRESENTATION

In Southeast Asia, meals are presented in aesthetically pleasing ways, even in poor households where pandanus or banana leaves substitute for the dishes made of precious metals or ceramics used in elite households. Finished side dishes of food are garnished with fresh aromatic herbs, fried onions, or even edible flowers. Plates, rice bowls, or shallow rimmed bowls are common ware in kitchens throughout the region, and vary from antique works of art, to products from local ceramic factories, to brightly colored plastic. The quality of the items used for food presentation separates elite or palace meals from village meals. The ceramic, basketry, and textile traditions of Southeast Asia produce presentation possibilities to rival any European dining room table setting. Artisans produce small low woven bamboo tables, woven baskets for sticky rice, textile hangings to separate dining areas from sleeping areas, and more recently for use as tablecloths; woven mats for seating and food display; and ceramic pedestal trays, lidded bowls, plates, and water bowls for drinking and washing. In the past, skilled metalworkers created silver, brass, and bronze utensils, pedestal trays, lidded bowls, and betel sets displaying delicate filigree work in floral designs. Export wares from China and Thailand moved throughout the region and surfaced in the palaces of distant kings and sultans. Celadon ware from Sawankalok, Thailand, dating back to the tenth century, was a particularly popular trade ware, with its distinctive glaze that fires to a lustrous pale green.

MEAL FORMATS

How are Southeast Asian dishes arranged into meals? Meals do not usually begin with appetizers, a European meal category recently adopted in urban centers for receptions where people stand while snacking and drinking. The western category of appetizer might better be understood as food paired with drinks—often snack foods purchased from street vendors or side dishes without rice. If rice is not served, then one is "eating for fun" rather than consuming a meal.

Southeast Asian meals are served all at once, rather than in courses, unlike Chinese meals that are served in a sequence of overlapping courses; in Chinese restaurants, one course need not be completely finished before

Hanoi noodle and vegetable lunch.

the next dish is brought to the table. While rice and soups should be served hot in temperature, side dishes may be served at room temperature, as small kitchens cannot make and serve all side dishes at the same time. This simultaneous presentation of all parts of the meal provides the eater with maximum choices about what tastes go best together. Each side dish served with rice tries to balance tastes. But it is the combination of side dishes into meals where more balance is achieved. Even then, people eating the meal create the final balance as they serve themselves from the available side dishes in the order they prefer, and fine tune tastes with wet or dry condiments, reflecting individual needs and desires.

While Westerners often associate peasant diets with monotonous meals and laud the diversity of North American meals, even poor families in Southeast Asian villages may eat a wide range of foods. One Malay villager consumed, in a seven-day period, four kinds of cake, two types of crackers, some wheat rolls, seven species of fish prepared in five different styles, a stew of clams and vegetables, six types of vegetables, and seven varieties of fruit in addition to rice.[1]

ELEMENTS OF SOUTHEAST ASIAN MEALS

What are the common elements of meals in Southeast Asia? First, rice (or in some cases another available starch such as maize or cassava) is the central core of most meals and is usually served from a common bowl. Rice has a soul, and is a gift of the ancestors; its quantity and quality, its taste and smell, is a matter of constant concern. Side dishes, literally referred to as "with rice" dishes, accompany rice, and are also served in common bowls for sharing. Lao PDR is the only country in Southeast Asia where glutinous rice is the preferred staple and consumed regularly at most meals. It is also grown in pockets in Burma, and in northern and northeastern Thailand where some groups like the Shan prefer glutinous varieties. In Vietnam, it is preferred by upland minority peoples and used for ritual foods, although it is no longer a staple of everyday meals for most Vietnamese.

Soups

Side dishes usually include soup as a meal component along with rice and other side dishes, rather than as a separate course. Soups can be as simple as a clear broth with very few easily available ingredients, treated as a palate cleanser, or a more complex soup made with a flavor paste (see chapter 3). Soups are served from a common bowl directly onto rice, or into individual bowls; from there they are spooned on rice. Most soups are fast cooking, keeping vegetables crisp and nutrients readily available. Soup, either a rice congee or a noodle soup such as *pho*, can also be a meal in itself—often for breakfast or a late-night snack. The famous tamarind-based soups are well known in Thai, Malay, and Vietnamese meals. Soups with a coconut base are more associated with palace cooking, as in this Thai favorite.

Coconut Chicken Soup (in Thai, *tom kha gai*)

4 cups stock

4 cups coconut milk

4 chicken breasts, sliced

2 pieces of galangal, 1 inch, split or sliced

4 tbsp fish sauce

4 chiles, sliced

4 wild lime leaves, deveined and torn

2 pieces of crushed lemongrass, about 2 inches

Bring the stock to a simmer and add chicken, galangal, lime leaves, and lemongrass. Cook 10 minutes or until chicken is cooked through. Add coconut milk, chiles, fish sauce; heat through and serve.

Curries

Every Southeast Asian language has distinctive terms for the richly flavored stewlike side dishes served with rice meals. Often these dishes are translated into English as "curries." The origin of the term is disputed; the word *kari* in Malayalam is often glossed in English as curry, however the referent is not always a dish with gravy, but rather a spicy meat or vegetable side dish (which may be wet or dry) served with rice. The word is also identified with the Tamil word for soupy sauces or, as in Kerala, sauces made with black pepper. Because the various mainland languages often use *curry* to translate the wide range of spicy dishes, thick soups, and stews that are served with rice, the term has been used here, since the word *stew* congers up an even more inappropriate analogy of potatoes and gravy. However, the term *curry* should not be associated with curry powder and the complex history of curry as an invented British dish of Indian origin. In Thai, these mixtures are referred to as *gaeng*, and cover a wide range of wet side dishes.

Curries are only one kind of wet side dish that might be served with rice. In Southeast Asia, the term *curry* generally refers to any dish made with a flavor paste, with or without coconut milk. Flavor pastes could be as simple as garlic, chiles, shallots, and salt, or extremely complex, as in the royal versions of Thai and Khmer curries. Dry spices are more common in the flavor pastes of Burmese, Malay, and Indonesian curries. Lao and Thai also make forest curries with complex flavor pastes but no coconut milk. Some curries are simply boiled with the appropriate flavor paste; other recipes fry the flavor pastes in separated coconut milk. All the cuisines of the region have their own versions of curries made from beef, chicken, pork, shrimp, and fish, with varied flavor pastes for each. Local cooks can tell from the fragrance when the curries are ready to receive other ingredients, and when they are ready to serve.

Vegetables, Salads, and Pickles

Westerners do not usually associate salads with Southeast Asian food. Malaysian chef Wan Ismail also admits his initial bias against salads when he was younger in his cookbook, *Simply Sedap! Chef Wan's Favorite Recipes*. But all national cuisines feature dishes of raw or blanched vegetables with complex dressings or dipping sauces. These salads are served as a side dish with rice, rather than as a separate course. The vegetables are cut up ahead of time in uniform-sized pieces and mixed and dressed at the last minute; the cutting is the most time-consuming part of making the dish.

Kerabu are Nyonya versions of Malay salads, probably of Minangkabau origin; they are composed of blanched or raw vegetables, and can be made with shrimp or chicken for a more substantial dish. Malay, Vietnamese, and Lao meals all serve wild or cultivated greens eaten raw with dipping sauces, many of which have specific medicinal values (peppermint, pennywort, watercress, papaya leaf).[2] Thai salad dishes called *yam* are often served with alcoholic drinks.

Mango Salad

Most countries have a version of mango salad; this version captures the essence of these salads.

4 sour mangoes

3 tbsp brown sugar

2 tbsp fish sauce

3 tbsp tamarind juice

2 tbsp finely chopped chile peppers

1 cup shredded lettuce

3 tbsp finely chopped roasted peanuts

3 tbsp dry-roasted coconut flakes

coriander leaves

Slice the mangoes into 1-inch matchstick-sized pieces. Heat the brown sugar, tamarind juice, and fish sauce to dissolve the sugar. When cool, add chiles, and mix with the mangoes and shredded lettuce. Garnish with peanuts, coconut, and coriander leaves.

There are Lao, Cambodian, and Vietnamese versions of this salad that use only green unripe papaya. Colonial influences may also be seen in the ingredients used in some Cambodian and Vietnamese salads—particularly mustard and homemade mayonnaise.

Rice and side dishes are often served with salty or sour pickles, prepared quite quickly. After drying vegetables in the sun for several hours, they are then mixed in vinegar and sugar or brine for a few days. These pickles alter the taste of individual mouthfuls of food, and contribute to the creation of a unique taste profile for a household or community. That is, Malay pickles differ from Cambodian or Vietnamese pickles.

Carrot and Radish Relish

This simple relish is a common accompaniment to Cambodian and Vietnamese meals.

2 cups bean sprouts

2 carrots

1 daikon radish (or amount equivalent to 2 carrots)

2 green onions

1 cup water

2 tbsp sugar

1 tbsp salt

1/2 cup white vinegar

Rinse and trim seed coats from bean sprouts. Cut carrots, radish, and green onions into matchstick-sized pieces. Combine water, sugar, salt, and white vinegar in a nonreactive pot, and simmer for a minute; then cool and pour over vegetables. Let stand for at least an hour before serving.

Condiments and Dipping Sauces

Throughout Southeast Asia, dipping sauces and condiments add zest to bland rice, stimulating appetites and tempting eaters to consume more calories from starchy staples. They are often served with a plate of raw or lightly steamed vegetables in Cambodia, Lao PDR, and Vietnam. These salsa-like sauces are referred to as *nam prik* in Thai, *sambal* in Malay and Indonesian, *jeaw* in Lao, and *nuoc* in Vietnamese. Often sauces are named individually without use of the general term for sauce. The most important sauces in Southeast Asian meals are the fish sauces discussed in chapter two. These sauces are served alone or as parts of more complex dipping sauces such as Vietnam's nuoc cham.

Spicy Fish Sauce

1/4 cup fish sauce

1 tbsp sugar

1/4 cup lime juice

1 clove minced garlic

1 minced chile

1 tbsp vinegar

1/2 cup water

Grind chiles and garlic to a paste, and add remaining ingredients. Stir to dissolve sugar. Adjust amounts of ingredients to personal taste.

With the early adoption of chile peppers, originally from Central America, Southeast Asian communities added chiles to sauces originally heated with local black, white, or green peppers. Across the region, there is a common range of ingredients used in varying amounts to make dry or wet condiments, including ginger, galangal, fish sauce, lemongrass, turmeric, red onions or shallots, garlic, coriander, tamarind, basil, and mint. (See chapter 2 for a list of common ingredients.) Each combination is unique to a region, community, or household. Some sauce dishes contain dry condiments consisting primarily of salt and chile peppers, and are not given to children. These, too, add taste contrasts to meals. Even the most basic dipping sauces of Southeast Asia can be transformed with ingredients from colonial kitchens. (Recall the dipping sauce made from Worcestershire sauce described in chapter one.)

Indonesian *sambals* are made from mashed salted chile peppers, fresh or fried, with or without shrimp paste and spices. In Lao and some Thai sauces, the chiles, garlic, and shallots are grilled before they are ground into pastes. These sauces keep well and appear with every meal. Many of the ingredients are similar to those used in making flavor pastes and marinades.

Drinks

Water is always served to guests but is not generally consumed with meals, but rather proceeding or following meals. Sugarcane juice and the juice from young coconuts are popular drinks available from street vendors. Diluted Chinese tea used to be served with restaurant meals in towns and cities, but coffee has become much more popular over the last few decades. Coffee and tea are often served with a layer of sweetened condensed milk. There is also a long history of tonic-like teas in many Southeast Asian countries. Carbonated beverages are available and popular everywhere in the region now, with Pepsi and Coca Cola often competing to monopolize the cola market in different countries. (Thailand is Coca Cola country, while Lao PDR is Pepsi country.)

Fermented rice liquor plays a key role in many non-Muslim celebrations, as consumption of alcohol creates links between the living and the dead, humans and spirits, and guests and hosts. Among minority groups living north of Luang Prabang, rice alcohol (*laolao*) is kept in heirloom jars, and in the past was a necessary ingredient for oath taking and other rituals. Producing *laolao* used to be a household enterprise, but more recently the liquor is purchased from local entrepreneurs who grow special glutinous rice specifically for this purpose. Steamed sticky rice is fermented with balls of yeast for about a week, when it is then distilled and consumed. Locally produced commercial beers including Beer Lao, Singha, San Miguel, and Tiger are popular with middle-class consumers and tourists. *Bia hoi,* the fresh draft beer introduced to Vietnam by the Czechs, provides an occasion for a unique social and taste experience, as people gather to drink the mild beer in the evenings. While rice wine has a long history, wine from grapes is usually imported and is a newly acquired taste, except in areas colonized by the French. Commercial distilleries in Thailand also produce local western-style whiskeys and gins.

Desserts and Sweets

Desserts are particularly popular in the islands of Southeast Asia, where *keuh-keuh* (*kuih-kuih* in Malaysia and Singapore) or sweets are enjoyed more as snacks than as the last course of everyday meals in most households. However, they have an important role in festive events and are a key component of courtly palace meals. Perhaps linked to Hindu rituals where sweets are important temple offerings, sweets symbolize all that is rich and joyous in the world, and are always given to guests.

Seasonal fruits are served both to end a meal and as snacks, as is fruit preserved in sugar, pickled fruit, sour fruit sprinkled with sugar, and dried

Vietnamese pancakes (kanom bueng yuan) with savory and sweet fillings, Salaya, Thailand, 2008.

fruit. Fresh fruit is always served peeled and beautifully cut in neat bite-sized pieces. One of the best-known accompaniments for seasonal fruits like mangoes is sticky rice with coconut milk (see recipe in chapter 2).

In addition to fruit, which is often considered a snack, Southeast Asian desserts can be grouped in a number of different categories: in Vietnam, sorbets and ice creams, dessert soups, cookies and cakes, sweetmeats, seaweed and rice, and items for special events; in Malaysian and Indonesian cookbooks, European-style baked goods, sweet puddings, and market sweets.[3] These categories reflect the wide variety of dishes that might fall into the western category of dessert. But there are many overlaps and surprises along the way.

Consider the overlap between drinks and desserts. Recent innovations like fruit smoothies, iced fruit drinks, and bubble teas link sweet drinks directly to certain classes of regional desserts. Traditional teas, tonics drinks, and desserts overlap in Malaysia, for example, where jasmine flower and sweet osmanthus teas are mixed with sugar, white fungus, Chinese pear, and red fig dates to make a cooling dessert that also cures coughs. *Ais kacang* is an iced dessert popular in Malaysia and Singapore, with close relatives in Thailand and the Philippines. It exemplifies the personification of dishes so popular in the region, as customers determine what goes into the dish, in addition to red beans, seaweed jelly (agar-agar), grass jelly (a jelly-like substance made from mint leaves), palm seeds, and corn kernels, all drizzled with palm sugar syrup and sweetened condensed milk, and served over shaved ice. Vendors offer additional choices of preserved and fresh fruits, canned fruit cocktail, aloe vera, and candies. The Philippine version is called *halo-halo* and includes a scoop of ice cream under the shaved ice, along with additional options including yam jam, sweet potato cubes, and chickpeas.

Ice cream—particularly coconut ice cream—is a popular dessert in the region; in Thailand, it is served in a bun with sweetened condensed milk, and in the Philippines, in *halo-halo* mixtures, with red beans or chickpeas. These are taste contradictions to many North Americans but are common in Southeast Asian desserts. This Burmese dessert porridge is another taste contradiction, for, like many Southeast Asian desserts, it uses salt to cut the sweetness.

Coconut Porridge

1/2 cup white rice

1/4 cup coconut milk

1/3 cup sugar

1/3 tsp salt

Soak rice in water for 30 minutes and drain. Boil uncovered with 5 cups of water for 25 minutes. Add coconut milk and sugar and simmer for 15 minutes. Add salt and serve with additional sugar or salt.

Other dessert or breakfast options include sweet puddings made with coconut milk, glutinous rice or taro flour, palm sugar, or sticky rice. Steamed rice and bananas wrapped in leaves and glutinous rice cakes are popular portable sweets. Firm jelly-like sweets in jewel colors can also be seen in markets throughout Southeast Asia, and are eaten as snacks, desserts, and in iced drinks. These fluorescent-colored treats with their rubbery textures are the least familiar to western palates.

More familiar to North American tastes are cakes and cookies. Where colonial powers stayed the longest, Southeast Asian desserts more closely resemble European baked goods made with butter, wheat flour, and sugar. However, local desserts may substitute rice flour or mung bean flour and palm sugar. Other substitutions reflect changing tastes; chicken eggs have replaced duck eggs, as white granulated sugar has replaced palm sugar in many desserts, giving them a different character recognizable to the older generation.

Bandung in Java has a legacy of 400 years of association with Dutch colonizers. The moist fluffy cakes and crisp cookies produced by local bakers there are spiced with ingredients like nutmeg, cinnamon, and cloves.

COMPOSING MEALS

Breakfast, lunch, and dinner are western categories but are useful for delineating the timing of meals. But the poorest households may not make these distinctions, and may eat very similar dishes for every meal. For them, meals are shaped by whether rice is cooked early in the morning, with leftover rice eaten at later meals, or cooked for an evening meal, providing leftovers for the next morning.

The Tai Yong, a Shan group living in northern Thailand, steam their glutinous rice once a day early in the morning. The late rice meal is served at dark between 6 and 7 P.M. In addition to the leftover sticky rice, frogs gathered in the rice fields might be cooked in a pot with green leafy vegetables and fermented fish and a flavor paste composed of salt, ginger, garlic, basil, mint, and coriander. The rest of the frogs might be deep fried with turmeric and lemongrass, and served with fresh coriander. Steamed greens gathered from the garden or forest that day would be served together with a hot chile dipping sauce.[4]

Farmers are likely to eat two rice meals a day, at dawn and dusk, and carry leftovers with them into the fields to eat at midday. A rural Lao family might sit down, morning or evening, to a basket of sticky rice; a bowl of *padek* (fermented fish paste); a plate of fresh greens including coriander, mint, basil, watercress, cannabis, lettuce, and wild greens from the forest with a chile-based dipping sauce; and a pot of fish soup with bamboo shoots.

Urban Vietnamese follow a three-meal pattern, with breakfast consisting of rice soup, noodle soup such as *pho*, sticky rice with mung beans, or baguettes. Lunch might be rice noodles in a café, with a dinner at home of rice, sour fish soup, a dish of stir-fried vegetables, fresh vegetables, and hot tea. Indonesian and Malay meals might be composed of a dry *sambal*, wet *sambal*, a vegetable stew or soup, a meat or fish dish, sliced cucumbers, crunchy condiments, and shrimp crackers. A Bangkok office worker might have to take breakfast on the run because of traffic problems, take a formal break for lunch at a food court, and consume a rice meal with the family in the evening.

Morning Meals

The habit of having noodle soups or rice congee for breakfast probably came from China and is an urban custom well entrenched in the cities of the region. Lao hotels offer three kinds of breakfasts—French, Lao, and American. French breakfasts include baguettes with butter, fruit, and coffee; Lao breakfasts consist of steaming bowls of rice porridge with pork, fish, or chicken, with condiments; American breakfasts offer eggs, bacon or sausages, toast, and coffee. Each option makes assumptions about how different people like to break their fast, and also reflects recent Lao history.

Burmese and Vietnamese markets are likely to offer glutinous rice dishes from food vendors prepared early in the morning since these specialized dishes take some time to prepare.

Sticky Rice with Hominy

This is a Vietnamese version of a breakfast dish.

2 cups glutinous rice

1 can white hominy

3/4 tsp salt

1 tsp sugar

1 cup cooked mung beans

1/3 cup crispy caramelized onions

2 tbsp toasted sesame seeds

Soak sticky rice overnight or for 6 hours. Rinse soaked rice in cold water, and put in a steamer with hominy. Steam for 20 minutes, adjusting and turning rice/hominy mixture once to ensure even steaming. Wash mung beans and simmer in water for 20 minutes until soft. Drain and set aside. Crush sesame seeds, salt, and sugar in mortar and pestle. Put rice on platter, add mung beans on top, and sprinkle with sesame mixture and fried onions. Food vendors offer other accompaniments, including coconut cream, roasted peanuts, coriander, sausage, and chopped green onions.

Lunch Noodles

Noodles, derived from Chinese versions made from rice or wheat flour, eggs, or mung beans, are everywhere is Southeast Asia. Rice or mung bean vermicelli are also known as glass noodles, and Chinese egg noodles as *mee*. Fresh or dried rice noodles come in several widths and are familiar lunch staples, served dry or in soup with fish or meat and vegetables. Fried noodles prepared by food vendors are available for early morning meals, provide complete midday meals in towns and cities, and at home can be integrated into the meal formats of family dinners.

Vietnamese urban workers carried lunches to work during the period of food rationing in the 1970s and 1980s. Today, workers order rice boxes from local restaurants to be delivered for lunch or dinner; restaurant workers return to pick up the plastic box to wash and refill for the next day's delivery.

Noodle dishes are easily borrowed, transformed, commodified, and personalized. New versions of noodles dishes are created and named by vendors and food courts as if they have long histories. For example, drunken noodles (*pat kii mao*) add Maggi sauce to a hot chile base. Sukhothai noodles use a spicy tamarind soup base with ground pork and green beans. The pattern of naming set versions of noodle soups seems better established in Malaysia, where asking for a dish like *laksa* gives one a standard recipe. But after the cook prepares the noodles to the customer's order, the customer makes further adjustments to the taste by adding wet or dry condiments.

Coconut Chicken Noodles

This Burmese-influenced dish, popular in northern Thailand, may have been brought to the region by Shan or by Haw Muslim traders from Yunnan. Whoever brought the dish to northern Thailand, it tastes wonderful. The Burmese version uses chickpea flour and is a special dish served at weddings and birthdays. Burmese refer to the dish as *kyauswe*, while Thai refer to it as *khaw soi*.

2 cloves garlic

1 tbsp red curry paste

1 tsp ground turmeric

1/2 lb stewing beef or 3/4 lb chicken thighs

3 cups canned or fresh coconut milk

1 tbsp sugar

1 cup water

2 tbsp fish sauce

Mince garlic and place in bowl with ground turmeric, pinch of salt, and curry paste. Stir-fry mixture in 1 tbsp oil and add 1/2 cup of thick coconut milk. Add meat and sugar and cook, stirring frequently, until meat is cooked. Add remaining coconut milk, water, and fish sauce and cook for 10 minutes. Ladle sauce and meat over cooked noodles divided into 4 bowls. Squeeze fresh lime juice over mixture. Garnish with fried noodles, sliced shallots, green onions, lime slices, pickled cabbage, and ground chili to taste. (Best over thin egg noodles.)

In Vientiane, one family near the National University of Laos offers a noodle dish for students and faculty who sit in the courtyard of their house and sample the noodles they used to make at home in Bokeo province. They identify the dish as Shan.

Bokeo Lao/Shan Noodles

1/2 lb ground pork

2 shallots

1 head garlic

3 hot chile peppers

3 tbsp fermented soybean paste

1/2 cup stock

2 tomatoes

1 tbsp oil

salt and black pepper to taste

lime slices and green onions

Fry finely chopped garlic and shallots in oil. Add bean paste, chiles, and ground pork, and stir-fry for 5 minutes. Add stock and tomatoes and simmer until sauce is reduced. Spoon over cooked noodles and garnish to taste with green onions and lime slices. (Best over medium-wide fresh rice noodles.)

With the availability of excellent low-cost baguettes in French Indochina, a special sandwich tradition developed in Vietnam and spread to Cambodia and Lao PDR. Best known by the Vietnamese term *banh mi,* the sandwich is available from street vendors in towns and cities.

Banh Mi

Sliced baguette

Mayonnaise

Sliced pate, sliced ham, or sliced sausage

Chiles to taste

Carrot relish

Soy sauce

Lettuce, tomatoes, and cucumber slices

Coriander

Spread split plain or toasted baguette with mayonnaise. Assemble sandwich with meats, relish, and other items, finishing with soy sauce and coriander.

Evening Meals

Electric rice cookers make evening meals less stressful and are appearing even in small villages with electricity; they are no longer elite urban technology. When family members work outside the home in cities like Bangkok, dinners at home may consist of rice prepared in an electric rice cooker and plastic bags of side dishes purchased from street vendors or supermarkets. These side dishes are both expertly prepared and very reasonable in cost. Bangkok traffic makes it less appealing to head out to restaurants or food courts after work. However, in cities like Penang, Singapore, or Phnom Penh, dining out is more easily accomplished in night markets where street vendors cluster together and can be reached easily without great traffic delays (as discussed in chapter 5).

Evening dinners are the most likely meal for serving elaborate dishes to go with rice—coconut-based curries, grilled fish, rich stews, and complex soups. Adobo is probably the best-known Philippine dish, representing both Philippine cooking methods and Spanish influence in the cuisine of the country. It is a stew made from beef, chicken, goat, lamb, vegetables, or seafood, and flavored with a vinegar, salt, and garlic base. As a staple of evening meals, the dish improves the longer it is kept.[5] It is analogous to the curries of mainland Southeast Asia, but without royal courts and the Indianized cuisines they introduced, Philippine cooking developed its own distinctive flavors.

Warfare in Vietnam, Cambodia, and Lao PDR disrupted traditional cooking practices for more that a decade, and many people experienced severe food shortages. With the return of peace and stable food markets, young people are relearning traditional dishes. This Vietnamese dish would go well with rice or vermicelli noodles.

Marinated Pork Tenderloin

Marinate pieces of pork loin or trimmed pork shoulder in the following marinade

1 tbsp sherry
2 cloves minced garlic
2 tbsp caramel sauce
2 tbsp soy sauce
1 tsp oil
1 tsp rice vinegar

Marinate pork in refrigerator for 6 hours, turning occasionally. Remove from refrigerator an hour before grilling or broiling. Preheat oven to 475 degrees, or prepare grill. Reserve marinade to baste. Roast or grill 30 minutes, turning occasionally. Rest 10 minutes and slice thinly against the grain. Serve with dipping sauces.

POVERTY MEALS, PALACE MEALS

Formal restaurants in the region and overseas primarily serve dishes first prepared in royal palaces—the food of the elite. These are the recipes that are most likely to have been written down. Most information is available about royal Thai and Khmer dishes, as well the imperial Vietnamese cuisine at Hue. Less information is available about the food served in the royal courts of Mandalay, for example. However, on analogy with the Buddhist kingdom of Luang Prabang, Lao PDR, it is likely that the food of peasants and kings did not differ that much in taste and meal format.

While the refined taste of the courts and the urban elite encouraged the development of special dishes, rural people and servants enjoyed the raw, strong, unrefined flavors of dipping sauces made from fermented fish products, used for dipping unripe fruit and garden vegetables. People of refined taste claimed to find the fermented fish pastes disgusting.[6] Peasant food is generally simple, fast to prepare, and makes use of local seasonal ingredients such as lotus stems, water spinach, gourds, eggplants, and aromatic herbs. In contrast, court food is elaborate, time consuming to prepare, and makes use of more expensive, rare ingredients.

It is important not to idealize or romanticize poverty dishes and meals consumed in poor Southeast Asian households and communities. Such meals might be characterized by what they lack—sufficient staples, protein sources, and variety. But they should not be ignored because they represent the everyday or typical meals for thousands of people in the region. Poor rural communities do not idealize foods "from the past" such as dried fish, insects, and fermented fish paste. Instead, as resources permit, families incorporate these items into modern diets that provide more diversity and better-quality meats. For example, chicken dishes that used to be made from feet and bones alone can include meatier parts of the bird when the meat does not have to be stretched so far.

Increasingly, rural farmers are relying on cash crops like garlic, cabbage, eggplants, or tobacco, and using the cash earned to buy rice. This model of agricultural diversity provides households with the potential for diverse diets. People without access to land or cash to purchase food consume the poorest meals. A poor Burmese farmer might be limited to a bowl of steamed rice with a little peanut oil and salt, accompanied by a small piece of dried fish. A poor Lao farmer might flavor his sticky rice with a dish of fermented fish (padek), fresh greens, and bamboo soup. Soups provide innovative ways to stretch meals to feed extra people in times of food shortages.

Water Spinach Soup

This Burmese soup could be made from any locally available greens.

1 large bunch of water spinach (or other quick-cooking greens)
6 cups water
2 tsp vegetable oil
1 chopped onion
2 cloves garlic
1/2 tsp ground turmeric
2 tbsp fish sauce
1/2 cup tamarind juice

Cut washed greens into bite-sized pieces. Heat oil and stir-fry onion, garlic, and turmeric. Add fish sauce, tamarind juice, and water. Bring to a boil, add spinach leaves, and simmer for 10 minutes.

Coconut-based curries with rare and expensive spices are characteristic of courts and palaces, and seldom appear in rural communities except on festive occasions when villagers celebrate in "royal style," behaving and eating as if they were royalty.[7] In all Southeast Asian countries, the most elaborate desserts are associated with royalty and elite meals. This is best known in the case of Thai and Khmer desserts. The origins of recipes are hard to determine, but there are hints of possible routes of influence. Cambodian sweets may have been influenced by recipes and products from Java, brought from Arab traders and Indian Brahmans. When the Siamese defeated the Khmer, they brought back Khmer cooks. Thus, Thai palace cuisine was probably influenced by the imperial cuisine at Angkor Wat. From there, dishes were further developed in the Ayuttaya courts, with the addition of Portuguese recipes during the reign of King Narai, and returned into the royal Khmer kitchens. Some of the most famous Portuguese-Siamese desserts were attributed to Mary Gimard, or Thao Thong Giip Ma, the Portuguese-Japanese wife of Constance Phaulkon, the Greek adventurer who became Prime Minister under King Narai of Ayuttaya (1656–1688). She was credited with adapting Portuguese egg-based desserts into special royal desserts including a custard served in squash and a complex sweet made to look like mango seeds.[8]

In the 1800s, Thai and Khmer palaces had separate kitchens for making desserts and snack foods. Women—wives, concubines, and members of the inner court—produced these luxurious, labor-intensive items. Palace desserts were feasts for the eyes as well as taste buds and included delicate carved fruits and vegetables, sugared flowers, perfumed water, and jasmine flowers picked at sunset, steeped in water overnight, and used to flavor sugar and finished desserts. Miniature fruits and vegetables known as *look choob*, made of soybean paste, palm sugar, and coconut, and dipped in gelatin, were once only found in the palace or served at "royal style" weddings. Over the last decade, these palace sweets have become available in supermarkets and served at receptions.

Vietnam had its own version of royal food, the imperial dishes of Hue. Here, vegetarian food was taken to new heights with the influence of Mahayana Buddhist monasteries. The imperial cuisine refined ordinary dishes and treated eating as an art, with more sophisticated cooking techniques and presentations—for example, dishes such as chicken soup with lotus seeds, crisp spring rolls, grilled pork in rice paper, and minced shrimp wrapped around sugar cane. Southern dishes included pungent beef in betel leaves and glutinous rice desserts formed in banana leaf

Food workers display palace dessert, *look choob*, for a Thai reception, 2008.

boxes. Imperial cuisine also made use of unusual ingredients such as green bananas or unripe figs, but all served in very delicate portions.[9] After years of food shortages, new food businesses are opening in Vietnam, and cooks are rediscovering the joys of cooking traditional dishes.

Urban–rural and palace–village contrasts often can be reduced to the food secure and the food insecure. On the other hand, it is often poor farmers working in marginal locations who have access to rare wild forest foods so valued by elite cooks. Of course, only the food secure can afford to be refined about their food choices. Overall, hearty peasant fare has made a greater contribution to the world's culinary knowledge than refined aristocratic recipes.

ICONIC DISHES, ICONIC MEALS

Typical meals are meals that are commonly eaten in Southeast Asia. But neither typical nor common are terms that help organize the diversity of meals consumed in the region. This section examines a few dishes that condense meaning and stand for more than themselves. Certain dishes become iconic of a region or country; that is, they come to stand for the diversity of food dishes in an area. Their iconic status may come about through external contact such as colonialism or tourism. But national governments may have a hand in the promotion of some dishes as typical, or the best the country has to offer. Such dishes may be promoted through World Fairs, trade expositions, food festivals, or heritage tourist sites.

Iconic foods are not necessarily elite foods, nor foods that are only served in urban restaurants. Consider hamburgers, for example, or gourmet macaroni and cheese—they are comfort foods that carry iconic meanings, as well as foods that translate well into being cooked in other kitchens. To conclude this discussion of typical meals, consider the dishes that signify national or ethnic identity, keeping in mind that what may be viewed by both insiders and outsiders as an iconic or marker food may in fact be part of an invented tradition.

The best-known iconic Southeast Asian meal is the rijstaffel or rice table, an invented meal that represents the Dutch colonial experience in Indonesia and is still reproduced in restaurants throughout the Netherlands. For many Europeans, this might have been their first exposure to the tastes of the region. Rijstaffel offers small dishes of meat, vegetable, and fish dishes along with sauces (sambal ulek), satay, and shrimp crackers (krupuk). Often plain rice and flavored, colored rice are both served, along with 30 or more small savory dishes and sauces. The larger the number of guests, the more dishes are served. Leftovers often taste better the next day and are served together as a miniature rijstaffel.

Some noodle dishes have reached iconic status, and almost stand for the nation where they are served: For example, Thailand's *pat Thai* (see recipe in chapter 5), Vietnam's *pho*, and Malaysia's *Penang asam laksa* noodle soup are treated as national dishes. The noodle dish *pat Thai*, a recent invention linked to Thai nationalism in the 1940s, has taken on a life of its own, appearing in Thai restaurants overseas and even as an entrée item in western restaurants. Instead of the wide range of fried noodle dishes available in Thai markets, outside of the region the choice of fried noodles is often limited to a single iconic dish, *pat Thai*.

The most typical soup served in Vietnamese households is a simple sour fish soup called *canh chua*. A staple of south and central Vietnam, it uses very fresh fish boiled in a tamarind fish stock seasoned with aromatic herbs, similar to the soup base for Vegetarian soup (see chapter 6). The soup condenses the elements of a Vietnamese meal in a single dish.[10] But it is the northern favorite, beef *pho* (see chapter 5), that most westerners know as a typical Vietnamese soup. Similarly, *banh Tet*, New Year's glutinous rice cakes, symbolize new beginnings for ethnic Vietnamese.

The best known Lao dish is *laap*, a spicy minced fish or meat dish served primarily on festive occasions in villages, but also served in restaurants in the country and overseas. This iconic dish condenses many significant contrasts; real men eat *laap dip*, raw *laap*, while women and those concerned about the health risks associated with eating raw meat prefer their *laap suk*, or cooked.

Beef Laap

This version is cooked lightly, but it could be modified for other taste preferences.

1 lb lean ground beef

1 green onion, finely chopped

2 chopped chiles

1-inch piece of galangal, finely chopped

2 stalks finely chopped lemongrass

1 tbsp fish sauce

2 tbsp lime juice

1 1/2 tbsp roasted rice powder

1/2 cup chopped mint

1/2 cup chopped coriander

Cook beef lightly in a nonstick pan and let cool. Mix with all other ingredients. Adjust seasonings to taste, and serve on a bed of lettuce with extra coriander and mint.

Malaysian foods often condense symbolic messages about hybridity in a multicultural society where everyone gets along and eats each other's food. Malaysia's long history at the crossroads of the spice trade required creating relations with western traders and colonizers. This is reflected in the country's ethnic complexity today. Dishes like *rojak*, Malay mixed salad, bring different things together in a single dish where the individual flavors are still identifiable. This dish, with its wide variety of fruits, vegetables, and shrimp paste holding it all together, has become a metaphor for the ethnic mix in Malaysia.

Nyonya dishes combining Chinese and Malay cooking traditions also express the diversity of Malaysian food. Curry Kapitan is described as an Indian dish made by a Chinese cook to serve to an English captain. It is a dish that is served in Nyonya restaurants in Penang as an exemplar of that tradition.

Chicken Curry Kapitan

1 chicken, cut in pieces (about 3 lbs)

3 cups coconut milk

1/2 cup grated coconut

1/2 cup tamarind water

1 lemon

3 tbsp oil

Flavor paste

10 dried chiles

10 fresh chiles

1 stalk lemongrass, minced

3 cloves garlic

6 shallots

selection of dried spices including 1 tsp each of nutmeg, coriander, cumin, cinnamon

1 whole star anise

Mash the flavor paste ingredients together. Grind dry spices to a powder and add to flavor paste. Brown the grated coconut in a dry pan. Cut chicken into serving-size pieces. Heat oil and stir-fry flavor paste until fragrant. Add chicken pieces and stir-fry until well coated. Add coconut milk and tamarind juice and simmer until chicken is cooked. Add ground coconut, salt to taste, and juice of a lemon. Garnish with fried onions and serve with rice.

Other iconic dishes are associated with particular places. In Malaysia, *Penang asam laksa* is a special noodle dish consumed for breakfast or lunch, and very much associated with the typical taste of Malaysian food. Even this named dish is identified as being Chinese-Malay in some restaurants, and real Malay in others, depending on the ingredients used. While it is similar to other noodle dishes in the region, the rice noodles in fish sauce with aromatic ginger, pineapple, and prawn paste is described as capturing the unique flavor of Penang, *rasa rasa* Penang.[11]

NOTES

1. Carol Laderman, *Wives and Midwives: Childbirth and Nutrition in Rural Malaysia* (Berkeley, CA: University of California Press, 1983), p. 32.

2. The appendix of Laderman's book, *Wives and Midwives*, has an appendix listing edible wild plants used in Malaysia.

3. These categories come from Andrea Nguyen's cookbook, *Into the Vietnamese Kitchen* (Berkeley, CA: Ten Speed Press, 2006), p. 281, and James Oseland's cookbook, *Cradle of Flavor: Home Cooking from the Spice Islands of Indonesia, Malaysia, and Singapore* (New York: W. W. Norton & Company, 2006), p. 340.

4. Ing-Britt Trankell, "Cooking, Care, and Domestication: A Culinary Ethnography of the Tai Yong, Northern Thailand," *Uppsala Studies in Cultural Anthropology* 21 (1995): 137.

5. Amy Besa and Romy Dorotan, *Memories of Philippine Kitchens* (New York: Steward, Tabori, and Chang, 2006), p. 36.

6. The author of the best-known Cambodian cookbook in English, Longteine de Monteiro, writes: "You have to keep in mind that for Cambodian people of refined taste, like my own family, it was unthinkable—disgusting, even—to eat uncooked *prahok*, and here I was heartily lapping it up while the rest of the household slept." Longeteine de Monteiro and Katherine Neustadt, *The Elephant Walk Cookbook* (Boston: Houghton Mifflin, 1998), p. 3.

7. I refer to rituals where ordinary people pretend to be royalty for the duration of wedding or ordination ceremonies as royal-style rituals. Royal-style food would be served at such events. See Penny Van Esterik, "Royal Style in Village Context: Towards a Model of Interaction Between Royalty and Commoner," in *Royalty and Commoner: Essays in Thai Administrative, Economic, and Social History*, vol. 15, ed. C. Wilson, C. Smith, and G. Smith, Contributions to Asian Studies (Leiden: Brill, 1980), pp. 102–117.

8. This sweet is called *met mamuang*. The recipe is available in the *Elephant Walk Cookbook* on page 277. Thai cookbooks have similar recipes. Kanit also refers to this dessert as a Thai specialty, but before that, a Khmer court specialty,

and before that a Portuguese specialty. Kanit Muntarbhorn, *Gastronomy in Asia*, bk. 1 (Bangkok: M. T. Press, 2007).

9. Trieu Thi Choi and Marcel Isaak, *The Food of Vietnam* (Singapore: Periplus Editions, 1997), p. 16.

10. The discussion of sour fish soup comes from Nir Avieli's unpublished PhD dissertation from the Hebrew University (2003), "Rice Talks: A Culinary Ethnography of Identity and Change in Hoi An, Central Vietnam."

11. This is the title of a book about the street foods of Penang by Lim Siang Jin (Georgetown: Briobooks, 2006).

5
Eating Out

In Southeast Asia, as in most parts of the world, the very best local food is found in households, not in restaurants. But all the countries have active traditions of street foods, take-out foods, and Chinese restaurants, as well as interesting places for drinks. This chapter reviews some of the region's opportunities for public eating away from home, including the newly developed popularity of Southeast Asian restaurants overseas. The chapter has an urban, middle-class bias, since those are the people who are eating out on a regular basis.

Southeast Asian meal formats encourage food sharing. There are few restrictions on food sharing beyond religious rules forbidding pork (for Muslims) and beef (for Hindus). Unlike South Asians, Southeast Asians are not required to only eat foods prepared in a certain way, or only with members of extended families, nor are there rules about men or women eating individually or communally in public. The boundary between public and private eating is further blurred in Southeast Asia, where women cook and sell food on the streets and in small restaurants almost as an extension of the kitchens where they feed their families. In Southeast Asia, women—including veiled Muslim women—dominate food markets, and have full access to public spaces.

Restaurants providing the local Burmese, Cambodian, Thai, Vietnamese, or Malaysian cuisine are very recent in Southeast Asia. While Chinese restaurants flourished in the cities over the last century, it was difficult to find local food in restaurants. In Burma, all the restaurants were either

Chinese or Indian. Today, Bangkok provides perhaps the largest range of restaurants for dining out. But in the 1960s, there were very few Thai restaurants in the city. The best known include Jit Pochana, Seefah, and Sorng Daeng, where visitors and middle-class Thai ate classic dishes, many from the palace tradition. Sorng Daeng opened in 1957 in its present location near government offices in Bangkok, and still operates today. Here one could eat a very high-quality *pat Thai* noodle dish served on a banana leaf, tasting very much like the dish served by street vendors in the back allies, but of course, much pricier.

Eating out for lunch is particularly common in urban areas like Bangkok where the traffic can be very slow and the workplace, very distant from home. A household survey in 1990 revealed that households spent nearly half their monthly food expenditure on prepared food taken home or eaten away from home.[1] Since 1990, consumption of prepared food has been steadily increasing as food quality and convenience has improved greatly, including in supermarkets where prepared food is sold along with ready-to-cook precut ingredients packaged with all necessary aromatic herbs and spices.

In the past, eating out was a visible marker of status, a practice limited to the wealthy; where to eat was often more important than what to eat among upper-class urbanites. Today, eating out is a necessity. During the reign of Thai King Chulalongkorn, also known as Rama 5 (1868–1910), public eating outside the household first became more common, primarily

Woman in Penang selects vegetarian dishes from a Tamil-Malay restaurant, 2008.

for men. In 1883, 57 rice and curry shops were registered in Bangkok, where rice and curry "cook shops" open all day provided quick meals for civil servants who had to report to work early in the morning and work long hours.[2]

STREET FOODS

Southeast Asia is famous for its street food. According to Streetfood (http://streetfood.org), 40% of the daily diet of urban consumers in the global south is street food. Southeast Asia probably exceeds that estimate. Across the countries of the region, street vendors provide special foods for early morning travelers and late-night revelers. Night markets in the towns and cities of Southeast Asia gather together a number of food vendors to facilitate late-night dining when the temperature is lower. Hawker or street foods are not always available in restaurants; they can best be enjoyed on the street. The preparation of some street foods may be too complex or labor intensive for restaurants, or may require special equipment, or the items may not appeal to enough people—but the items can always be sold on the street. The mostly male hawker tradition in Singapore may have developed from the Straits of Malacca pattern of providing inexpensive meals to Chinese male manual workers.[3] A typical urban food market might have Muslim men selling satay and *roti*, Chinese women selling noodles, and young rural migrant women with baskets of fresh produce, including rare forest mushrooms. There is an almost-infinite variety of foods available on the streets; on a walk down the streets of Penang, Chiang Mai, or Hanoi at different times of the day one might encounter skewers of chicken, beef, or pork satay; sausages, sweet or savory roti; fried bananas; glutinous rice cakes; grilled squid; fried or fresh spring rolls; dumplings; fried locusts; salty or sweet fried doughnuts; crushed ice desserts; warm soybean milk; hot ginger tea; noodle soups; and rice porridge. Even roast suckling pig was available on the streets if you knew where to find it. (In Bangkok, look in Jatujak Park and under the expressway at Rama 3 road.)[4]

More recently, special royal-style desserts such as miniature fruits made of bean paste, formed into fruit shapes, colored, and dipped in jelly, can be purchased from street vendors in Bangkok. Small Vietnamese pancakes with sweet or salty fillings and *khanom krok*, coconut puddings made in special trays, competed for sale on the street with sweet pastry buns filled with vanilla and chocolate custard that appeared suddenly in the 1960s, imitations of the innovative dessert introduced into expensive Chinese restaurants in Bangkok.[5]

Food vendors often clustered around certain streets such as Lane 38, Sukhumvit Road in Bangkok, in the French quarter of Hanoi, and around housing estates in Singapore. Beside their small carts, some vendors provide the shade of an umbrella and small plastic tables and stools. The vendors share the same characteristics no matter where they appear; they provide the cheapest possible food and are well integrated into their neighborhoods, providing meals for manual workers, take-out side dishes for busy mothers, and snacks for everyone.

Vietnam, like Lao PDR and Cambodia, suffered from extremes of food insecurity during and after the American war. People in the north in particular suffered food deprivation, poverty, and malnutrition. Under conditions of food rationing, there was no pleasure associated with eating in such an ascetic regime with no street vendors and no open-air restaurants. As an overseas Vietnamese informant explained:

Our bodies and spirits were crushed then. It was a hunt for food every day. . . . Our food became more and more basic—rice and fish sauce if we were lucky. Everything had no taste. And now we can get anything we want from anywhere in the world. . . . And the food is so varied, so abundant, so fresh. This morning in the market, I could smell the green mangoes from the South. It was like heaven. My mother is teaching me recipes her mother taught her when she was a child—she had forgotten them until now because there was no food to cook with.[6]

Food is once again a pleasure for overseas Vietnamese and for Vietnamese in Vietnam where food vendors sell their popular noodle soup, *pho,* on the street. North Americans are more likely to have tasted *pho* noodle soup, made by Vietnamese immigrants, than the wide range of noodle soups popular in other countries of Southeast Asia. As with other dishes sold on the street, housewives make use of street vendors to avoid the hours of preparation and simmering necessary to make a rich broth for *pho.* In Lao PDR, *pho* is served with platters of fresh vegetables and greens to be eaten on the side or submerged in the hot soup.

Beef Pho

There are many versions of this satisfying rich soup. This recipe is characteristic of the soups available in the north of Vietnam. For a rich beef broth, use:

4 lbs beef bones with marrow (ox tails, shanks)

1 lb flank steak or beef shank

2 onions

1 tbsp salt

2 stalks lemongrass cut in 3-inch pieces

2 star anise

green onions

1 lb dried rice noodles

Soak bones overnight. Parboil beef bones for 10 minutes, and skim off surface fat. Rinse bones and set aside. Brown chopped onions in oil, and add sliced boneless beef. Add 6 quarts of water and the reserved beef bones. Add salt and lemongrass and simmer for 1 hour. Remove sliced beef and set aside. Continue simmering the stock for several hours, and strain out solids.

Meanwhile, boil dried rice noodles for 5 minutes, or follow package directions. Do not overcook. Drain and rinse with cold water. To assemble, bring the clear broth back to a boil. Divide noodles among soup bowls; top with sliced beef and green onions, and ladle hot broth over the noodles and beef. Garnish with hot chile sauce. Assemble a plate of salad greens and garnishes to accompany the soup, including lime slices, mint leaves, basil leaves, coriander leaves, chiles, bean sprouts, shredded lettuce, sliced cucumber, and other fresh seasonal greens.

Many Southeast Asian cities have tried to outlaw street vendors. Chinese and indigenous food available on the streets of Penang, Singapore, Hanoi, and Rangoon in the late colonial period was considered unclean by westerners. As early as the 1930s, colonial governments tried to control hawking and limit it to fixed places. When food was excluded from the streets and placed in government food centers, as in Singapore in the 1980s, it became more expensive. In cities like Penang, food vendors were regulated more closely and encouraged to congregate in one spot. Today, cities like Bangkok, Kuala Lumpur, Penang, and Singapore offer food courts in large air-conditioned shopping centers where health officials can more easily monitor cleanliness and food safety.

TAKE-OUT/TAKE-HOME MEALS

Street food vendors serve another important function in Southeast Asian cities: They provide take-away meals for busy families. The vendor's specialty can be wrapped in banana leaves, newspaper, styrofoam trays, or plastic bags for easy transport home. The appropriate condiment, dipping sauce, or pickle will also be put in a small plastic bag and shut tightly with a rubber band, ready to be placed in a suitable serving dish at home. Even soup can be taken away in these ubiquitous and very environmentally unfriendly plastic bags. In some communities, a *pinto*, or portable layered tray derived from the Indian-style tiffin carriers, makes take-out service even more convenient. It is also possible to order the ingredients and condiments from a vendor and assemble the dish oneself at home.

In 1998, a survey of the Greater Bangkok area recorded daily food expenditure on prepared foods taken home and found that nearly 70% was spent on rice and curry dishes, over 16% on noodles, and nearly 6% on fried rice. Less than 1% was spent on other prepared food, which may include some Western-style fast food.[7] Although McDonald's, Kentucky Fried Chicken, Dunkin' Donuts and other Western fast food outlets are franchised through large agri-food conglomerates, they have not displaced local fast foods that offer better value for money. The taste complexity of Southeast Asian foods makes Western fast foods less appealing except to teenagers seeking a comfortable place to hang out. Nevertheless, there are more than 100 McDonald's restaurants in Thailand, Malaysia, Singapore, and the Philippines, and none in Burma, Cambodia, Lao PDR, or Vietnam, a difference that reflects more on the penetration of capitalism than on local taste preferences.

Even smaller-scale food businesses dot the towns of Southeast Asia. Itinerant peddlers ply their specialties on bicycles or boats in residential areas in the evening, with customers coming out of their houses, often in nightclothes, and squatting or sitting on tiny low stools for one last bowl of duck noodles or rice porridge before bed.

MOBILE FOOD

Travelers—local and foreign—always have to eat out. Low-cost restaurants cluster around bus and train stations to serve "fast food" to travelers. Inside bus and train stations, other kinds of food are provided. This mobile food includes such items as sticky rice roasted in a bamboo tube, boiled eggs, dried fish, Chinese-style sausages, boiled corn, fried bananas, and satay (grilled meat on a stick). These food items travel well and are often wrapped in biodegradable banana leaves. Plastics are rapidly replacing banana and pandanus leaves, and they clog up roadside ditches near bus and train stations.

Pilgrimage is an important motivation for travel, and food features prominently in the event. Precooked food is often available at the foot of pilgrimage sites such as famous temples—Doi Sutep in Chiang Mai, Shwedagon in Rangoon, Burma, and the mosques and temples on Penang Hill. Here, meals can be consumed on the spot, picnic style, or taken home. Vendors provide a wide range of dishes to go with rice, designed to meet the tastes of visitors from different regions.

Hotels played an important role in the development of restaurants in the cities of Southeast Asia. Famous hotels that served colonial travelers and wealthy locals served a combination of Chinese and western food.

Mobile food vendor in Hanoi, 2008.

The Railway Hotel in Hua Hin, the Raffles in Singapore, the E&O in Penang ,and the Strand in Rangoon were justly famous for providing "civilized" British-style dining experiences for their customers.

During the reign of Rama 6 (1910–1925) hotels were the only places in Bangkok that served western food and drinks. Some of the famous old hotels include the Oriental, the Trocadero, and the Royal Hotel. Most five-star hotels in large Southeast Asian cities have special Chinese restaurants in addition to European restaurants. The Ambassador Hotel on Sukhumvit Road was one of the first of the Bangkok hotels to set the trend for having a special Chinese restaurant on the premises in the 1970s. These hotel restaurants provided locations for elite weddings. Later, the Ambassador Hotel democratized eating out by developing a public food court where locals and tourists could sample food from a variety of different locations in Thailand and elsewhere. Side by side, vendors sold specialties from northern, northeastern, and southern Thailand, Muslim dishes, coconut ice cream, and Italian pasta. The food offered was considered of higher quality than the same dishes sold on the street. Prices were slightly higher and the food preparation was more carefully regulated. With the involvement of hotels in food courts came more of an effort to regulate street foods yet make them available to visitors.

Today, food courts are available in shopping malls throughout the country and in neighboring Malaysia. Popular with tourists and locals alike, the customer buys redeemable coupons and uses them as cash to purchase a wide range of dishes from a selection of food vendors. The vendors then redeem the coupons and pay a percentage to the owner of the food court space. Food critics include food stalls and vendors in their published guides to good eating, such as the Shell Food Guide, to alert travelers and locals to the best food in Bangkok.

CHINESE RESTAURANTS IN SOUTHEAST ASIA

In Southeast Asia, Chinese restaurants, both in and outside of China-towns, provided the preferred cuisine for eating out. Chinese-owned res-taurants were much more common than shops selling local foods in most Southeast Asian cities. In Bangkok, Chinese restaurants are still the most popular locations for special meals consumed out of the house. In the past, Chinese-owned "cook shops" were the first places where Chinese and western cooking styles merged. Chinese food served with bread and butter was more likely to be offered in restaurants run by Hainanese families; such fusion would be unthinkable in Cantonese restaurants. Chinese restau-rants were the first in the region to serve set menus of Western food—soup, bread and butter, main course (pork chop), and cake. Today the modern yuppie restaurant in a Southeast Asian city is more likely to be Japanese or Italian than the old-fashioned Chinese version of western food.

It is often difficult to distinguish between Chinese food and regional food in small restaurants in the towns and cities of Southeast Asia because many cuisines in the region have borrowed techniques and recipes from Chinese food traditions, particularly noodle dishes and chicken, duck, or pork served on rice. In addition, there are multiple regional traditions of Chinese food that have had distinct impacts at different times and places in the region. Most food businesses were owned by Chinese immigrants to Thailand, Malaysia, and Cambodia, as well as other countries of South-east Asia. In addition, Sino-Thai, Sino-Lao, Sino-Khmer, and Nyonya (Malay-Chinese mix) all have their own distinct food traditions. Nyonya food is the heritage of early Chinese traders who came to Malacca, married local Malay women, and became wealthy from their businesses. Nyonya cuisine in Penang and further south is consciously promoted as distinct from both Chinese and Malay cuisine in the region.

Most cities in Southeast Asia have well-defined Chinatowns in addi-tion to restaurants owned by Chinese. Rangoon has Chinese restaurants in Chinatown, but few restaurants offering Burmese food. Bangkok had a number of famous Chinese restaurants including Golden Dragon, Tong Kee, and New Grand Shanghai, most serving southern Chinese food. Northern Chinese cuisine, including the famous Peking duck, is still harder to find in Bangkok.

Owner of one of the oldest Nyonya restaurants in Penang, 2008.

Ideally, eating out in a special Chinese restaurant involves 8–10 people and a sponsor or host—a format that is perfect for business meetings, but less suitable for courtship. For example, dishes such as Peking duck, steamed whole fish, or roast suckling pig are meant to be shared and are not suitable for individual small portions. A meal at a Chinese restaurant is likely to be more expensive than a European meal, or a local Burmese or Khmer meal, and is therefore considered more prestigious. Dim sum meals, where diners select small dumplings or similar items from trolleys, are more moderate in price and are popular for family meals on weekends. The format allows children to choose their own items, and the cost is substantially lower than at a restaurant serving a multi-course Chinese meal. For example, a specialty like shark fin soup is very expensive, and might cost ten times what a local soup would cost; but the best Chinese restaurants in Southeast Asian cities still provide a top-quality product. Today, a "Chinese table" meal of nine courses is too expensive for most middle-class families, although Sino-Thai or Chinese Malay enjoy Chinese style banquets for weddings.

While it may be possible to distinguish a Chinese meal from a non-Chinese meal, it is more difficult to try and distinguish Chinese dishes from local Southeast Asian dishes because the Chinese have resided in Southeast Asia for centuries and have adapted their traditional dishes to the tastes and ingredients of their new homelands. Dishes like stir-fried vegetables are true hybrids, and Chinese restaurants have adapted to local tastes with the use of coriander root, tamarind paste, and chiles in some places, and lemongrass or turmeric in others. But there have been times where an attempt has been made to distinguish between a Chinese and a local regional dish for nationalistic purposes. For example, *pat Thai* (Thai fried noodles) is a dish invented in the 1940s in Bangkok in an attempt to distinguish Thai noodles from Chinese noodles, and to encourage Thai civil servants to eat local.

Pat Thai is recognized as one of the favorite Thai dishes of foreigners visiting Thailand, and is perhaps most popular in Thai restaurants overseas. But it is only one of many fried noodle dishes available in Thailand. Perhaps its popularity with foreigners is due to the fact that it can be ordered by name in restaurants and from street vendors without the need to speak Thai. Ordering other Thai noodle dishes requires a long dialogue: Do you want your noodles thin, medium, or wide? Wet or dry? With beef, shrimp, or chicken? (And many Westerners prefer their noodle soup without intestines.)

Thai Fried Noodles, *Pat Thai*

A dry stir-fried noodle dish well known outside of Thailand, *pat Thai* is usually accompanied by bowls of chile-vinegar sauce, dried chile flakes, lime slices, chopped peanuts, sugar, bean sprouts, and sliced cucumbers, and decorated with coriander.

1/2 lb dried rice noodles, soaked in warm water 20 minutes

2 oz thinly sliced tofu (a 2-inch cake)

2 oz thinly sliced pork

1 tsp sugar

1 tbsp tamarind juice (or pulp squeezed from tamarind soaked in 2–3 tbsp warm water)

1 tbsp soy sauce

1 tbsp fish sauce

2 eggs

3 tbsp oil

2–3 cloves minced garlic

2 cups rinsed bean sprouts

1 tbsp dried shrimp

3 green onions cut in 1-inch pieces

Toss pork slices with sugar. In a small bowl, mix the soy sauce, fish sauce, and tamarind sauce. Lightly beat eggs with a pinch of salt. Stir-fry the garlic, pork, and tofu in a tablespoon of oil. Pour in egg mixture until it starts to set, and remove to a plate. In the remaining oil, stir-fry the drained noodles until they are well heated and seared. Add to the center of the wok the bean sprouts, green onions, dried shrimp, and the soy sauce mixture. Mix in the egg and pork mixture. Turn out on to a platter or individual plates and garnish with an assortment of the condiments listed above.

DRINKS

Thai, Lao, Cambodian, and Vietnamese cuisines offer a wide variety of foods that are considered ideal for accompanying drinks like whiskey or beer. Khmer and Lao favorites are typically "male" foods, such as fried or grilled meats, sausages, deep-fried snacks, and insects such as crickets and grasshoppers. Teahouses are very popular in Burma, where tea and coffee is served with a simple Indian-style bread. Traditional Burmese tea salad is very different from British notions of afternoon tea, and must have surprised a few colonial expatriates expecting cucumber sandwiches! Tea salad (*lephet-thoke*) is made from young tea leaves treated with salt and sesame oil and mixed with fried garlic, beans, split peas, roasted peanuts and sesame seeds, and fresh chiles.[8] Spoonfuls are scooped up and eaten along with cups of strong, bitter Burmese tea.

Coffee shops are becoming much more common in Southeast Asia. In Vietnam, local shops feature the newly available Vietnamese coffees. Thailand, too, has local franchised coffee shops. The *kopitiams* (Hokkien for coffee shops) have a long history in Malaysia, where Chinese immigrants had a monopoly on beverage sales and rented out space to other food vendors. They are examples of cosmopolitan spaces—neither home nor work—where people can gather, relax, and unwind without spending much money.[9]

THE EXOTIC EXTREMES

Few restaurants cater to exotic extremes, but in tourist centers like Bangkok or Singapore, the most unusual restaurants do a good business. Tum Nak Thai in Bangkok claimed to be the world's largest restaurant; servers on roller skates navigated the 10-acre site that served 3,000 people with classic Thai dishes in a garden setting enhanced with lights, water features, and flowers. The restaurant closed following the financial crisis of 1997. Other popular examples of extreme eating include seafood restaurants where customers choose their own fish from tanks with live fish swimming in them.

More adventurous tourists head to restaurants where items that are rare, expensive, or illegal are served. Snake, crocodile, tiger, bear claw, monkey brain—food that is considered rare or rapidly disappearing is served for a very high price.[10] The crocodile farm in Samut Prakan province provides crocodile meat to wild meat restaurants in Bangkok and to some Chinese restaurants that appeal to Chinese tourists. Animals such as the Bengal monitor used to be a preferred meat at the turn of the century, but this meat, like turtle meat, is no longer popular or widely available.[11] Another exotic meat advertised as increasing in popularity is rat. Rats from rice fields are drowned and sold at roadside booths, earning money for rural entrepreneurs and ridding villages of rats.

Insects are a necessity for their protein in some areas, an exotic luxury in others. For example, fried grasshoppers sold in street stalls in some parts of Bangkok provide protein for poor rural migrants and get rid of pesky grasshoppers. Called *rot duan*, or express train, in Thai, this dish is popular in markets in the north and northeast of Thailand and Lao PDR, along with giant red ants and water bugs, which are rainy season treats.[12]

TOURISM AND FOOD

Thailand was the first country in Southeast Asia to develop mass tourism, with help from the World Bank. In Bangkok in the 1960s, a variety of foreign restaurants opened in areas frequented by diplomats and foreign businessmen. Near Sukhumvit Road, where many foreigners lived, Korean, Lebanese, German, Japanese, Italian, French, and Mexican restaurants opened partly to meet the needs of the American military in Thailand. While some restaurants hired European chefs, others used local Chinese chefs who cooked food according to their perceptions about European food and what they thought Europeans and Americans liked to eat.

In the late 1960s, "authentic" Thai food was primarily available to visitors in the expensive classical Thai dinner and dance shows. Here, the staged authenticity of old Siam greeted both wealthy tourists and official visitors. Relaxing on royal silk cushions, and using bronze cutlery and *bencharong* (elaborate polychrome pottery) serving ware, both Thai and foreign guests ate royal dishes in a palace-like setting, replicating the late Chakri dynasty high culture of "Old Siam" and enjoying the perquisites of

elite royal palace culture. Part of the pleasure for tourists was being treated
not just royally, but *as* royalty, with luxurious consumption, servants, and
an emphasis on sensuous pleasure.[13]

With mass tourism, backpackers frequented special tourist restaurants
in towns like Vang Vieng in Lao PDR and the Khao San area of Bangkok,
where dishes such as American fried rice were served. American fried rice
comes with many stories of origin—one, that it was made with tins of
Libby canned vegetables; another, that it was fried with ketchup topped
with a fried egg, sausage, and Spam (a World War II–era canned processed-
meat product made from ground pork and spices). Most of these stories are
fueled by the availability of cans of Spam and Libby's mixed vegetables
"falling off the provisioning trucks" bound for American military bases in
Southeast Asia. Apart from American fried rice, attempts to feed tourists
what they wanted produced tourist dishes with more sugar, fewer chiles,
and salt instead of fish sauce.

Since the 1990s, food courts give tourists full access to a wide range of
local foods. Those dishes considered suitable for tourists are often identified in English. They include dishes that have been made popular by
Thai restaurants in Thailand and overseas—*tom kha ga* (chicken coconut
soup), *gaeng masaman* (spicy beef curry), chicken cashew, mixed vegetables, and *pat Thai*.

All-you-can-eat hotel buffets are of great appeal to hungry, somewhat
curious tourists. Buffet tables are usually works of art, featuring dozens of
Asian and European dishes side by side. Buffets give tourists both effi-
ciency and excess, and the opportunity to sample many different dishes—
foreign or local—and control the degree of "hot" or "exotic" they prefer.
The hotel buffet means that proprietors do not need to know exactly what
foreigners would like to eat, but need only supply them with all possible
options at a reasonable price.

CULINARY TOURISM

Recently, in its bid to attract "quality tourists," Thailand has developed
new strategies to attract tourists, including culinary tourism. Through
short courses and extended tours, visitors are provided with access to recipes for both royal palace cuisine and rural dishes. Since 1986, the Oriental Hotel has offered the first English-speaking Thai cooking school in
Bangkok, and probably in the country. In 1992, a visitor would pay $400
U.S. for five three-hour classes. Now a four-day cooking school experience costs $2,200 per person with accommodation at the Oriental Hotel
and most meals.[14] The recipes retain the essence of authentic Thai flavors;

salty flavor is provided by dried shrimp, fish sauce, or shrimp paste; sour, by vinegar, tamarind, and limes, the vinegar most familiar to European cooks; and spiciness by a range of herbs, peppercorns, and chiles. Students receive a certificate at the end of the course, recognizing them as Thai chefs. The purpose of such a cooking course was basically to show off Thai culinary skills and allow the students to order a wider range of authentic dishes in Thai restaurants.[15]

David Thompson, who runs a Michelin-star Thai restaurant in Australia, hosted a culinary tour to three Thai resorts in Bangkok, Chiang Mai, and Samui Island. Thompson claims to have documented traditional recipes and culinary techniques and will teach these in "beguiling locations." He locates Thai authenticity in the past and in the palace tradition: "Thai cuisine reached its apex in the last decades of the 1800s" in court food, where there is a balance of taste and textures. His restaurants are "devoted to authenticity," and his food is "triumphantly Thai," according to the *Bangkok Post* (January 14, 2005). When asked if he would open a restaurant in Thailand, he declined, saying Thai would pay top dollar for French or Italian food, but not for Thai food. Locals know they can get just as good food on the streets or in small restaurants for much less money.

In a country like Lao PDR that is food insecure, one might not expect great restaurants. But in cities like Vientiane and Luang Prabang, wonderful French restaurants are to be found, with Lao chefs trained in the French culinary arts. Many gourmet restaurants are relatively new on the scene and cater to the newly developed tourist market in the country. Young tourists are often attracted to eating sticky rice with their hands. But Lao cuisine is not as well known as Thai or Vietnamese. For example, the Sino-Lao owner of Keo's Thai Restaurant in Honolulu described Lao cuisine as crude and rustic compared to Thai or Vietnamese cuisine. It is certainly less sweet and features more bitter herbs. Lao cuisine is harder to replicate outside of Lao PDR because of its reliance on aromatic herbs that are rarely imported or grown outside of the country. Many greens and herbs are wild forest foods gathered by villagers and consumed immediately.

SOUTHEAST ASIAN RESTAURANTS OVERSEAS

For many westerners, Southeast Asian cuisine is equated with the food served in Thai restaurants in North America and Europe. There are currently around 20,000 Thai restaurants overseas, not all of them serving "authentic" Thai food. In 1976, there were 9 Thai restaurants; in 1999 there were 5,000, nearly half in North America.[16]

The Thai government has discovered that foreigners like Thai food, and they hope to use this affection to encourage tourism and deepen relations with other countries. The government can make it easier for foreign restaurants to import Thai foods, hire Thai cooks, and receive loans to open Thai restaurants abroad. As part of the promotion of Thai food as a healthy cuisine, the Thai government also attempts to standardize the taste and authenticity of Thai food.

Many Thai restaurants overseas have modified their dishes to suit what they assume are western tastes. They may use more soy sauce and less fish sauce, more red and green bell peppers and fewer hot chile peppers, and add unusual ingredients like maple syrup, olive oil, and peanut butter to stir-fry dishes.

The first Thai restaurant in North America was operated out of the Thailand Pavilion at the 1964 World's Fair in Flushing, New York. There they served *gaeng masaman* (beef curry with potatoes and peanuts) and *mii grop*, a puffy fried noodle dish that is seldom served in North America. People were attracted to the exotic tastes and the spiciness of the cuisine. The Malaysian booth served satay and Tiger beer to introduce Malay cuisine to North Americans.

One of the earliest Thai restaurants to open in North America was Keo's; it opened in Honolulu in 1977 under its first name, Mekong. The owner came from Laos before the revolution in 1975, bringing with him a model of Thai/Lao cuisine not available in his hometown of Vientiane. Although there is a close similarity between Thai and Lao language, culture, and religion, he explains the differences in the food: "I felt that Laotian food would not have been successful in America at that time. Laotian food is very basic and simple, and Thai food is very exotic and colourful."[17]

The economic boom of the 1980s resulted in a dramatic increase in the number of restaurants in Bangkok and overseas. Under conditions of globalization, more people have now tasted the flavors of Southeast Asian food, and have therefore come to expect these tastes to be available in gourmet restaurants around the world. Single dishes such as *pat Thai* or satay appear as entrée choices in international and fusion restaurants. And the flavors of lemongrass and tamarind are now available in grocery shops throughout North America, thanks to the increase in Lao, Vietnamese, and Cambodian immigration to North America between 1975 and 1985.

Although eating in restaurants is more common in urban areas, that does not mean that rural villagers and upland tribal peoples do all their eating in their own households and do not eat communally in public. Rather such meals are better described as communal feasts or ceremonies where food and eating has an important ritual meaning, the subject of chapter 6.

NOTES

1. Report of the 1990 Household Socio-economic Survey, cited in Giselle Yasmeen, *Bangkok's Foodscape: Public Eating, Gender Relations, and Urban Change* (Bangkok: White Lotus, 2006), p. 73.

2. Thanes Wongyannava, "Chinese Restaurants in Bangkok," in *The Transformation of Chinese Haute Cuisine in Bangkok's Chinese Restaurants* (research report, Toyoto Foundation, 2000), p. 10.

3. Yasmeen, *Bangkok's Foodscape*, p. 180.

4. Wongyannava, chap. 4, p. 5.

5. Wongyannava, "The Ever-Changing World of Food," in *The Transformation of Chinese Haute Cuisine*, p. 15.

6. M. Thomas, "Transitions in Taste in Vietnam and the Diaspora," *Australian Journal of Anthropology* (April 2004): 4.

7. Yasmeen, *Bangkok's Foodscape*, p. 209.

8. Chan, Susan. *Flavors of Burma* (New York: Hippocrene Books, 2003), p. 189.

9. Gaik Cheng Khoo is currently researching the kopitiam as cosmopolitan space in Malaysia.

10. Lisa Heldke discusses the wild animal market in Thailand in her book, *Exotic Appetites* (New York: Routledge, 2003), p. 75.

11. Wongyannava, "The Ever-Changing World of Food," in *The Transformation of Chinese Haute Cuisine*, p. 2.

12. Wongyannava, "The Ever-Changing World of Food," in *The Transformation of Chinese Haute Cuisine*, p. 5.

13. In *Materializing Thailand* (Oxford: Berg Press, 2000), p. 125, I argued that these classical dance shows were part of the process of marketing the invented tradition of "Old Siam" for tourists. The seductive appeal of Thailand is also made visible on tourist brochures and postcards.

14. I discuss these cooking classes at the Oriental Hotel in "From Marco Polo to McDonald's: Thai Cuisine in Transition," *Food and Foodways* 5, no. 2 (1992). Since that time, many more cooking schools have opened. However, culinary tourism is characteristic of Thai tourism, not of Southeast Asian tourism in general.

15. Susan Enfield, "Learning Thai Cooking in Thailand," *New York Times*, September 6, 1992.

16. "EXIM Thailand Expands Support to Thai Restaurants Overseas," newsroom, Export-Import Bank of Thailand, July 11, 2005. As part of their "Kitchen of the World" campaign, the Export-Import Bank of Thailand has been monitoring the success of Thai restaurants overseas. See also newsroom report for March 8, 3005.

17. Keo's Thai Cuisine, http://keosthaicuisine.com/gallery/gallery-cover-html.

6

Special Occasions

This chapter examines the occasions when people eat special food together. These include ritual events such as feeding the spirits of rice and one's ancestors, Buddhist and Muslim rituals involving food, rites of passage, and universal celebrations around the coming of the New Year.

In Southeast Asia, food creates and maintains social relations between people, and between people and the spirit world. Feeding others occurs across all transitions in the life cycle, and across all generations. Those who sponsor feasts gain status from feeding others appropriately and generously. In Southeast Asia, it would be unthinkable to celebrate without food. Most celebrations have a religious or ritual component to them, but purely secular celebrations also involve food. While Europeans may have viewed ritual feasting as leisure when they first came in contact with the region, participation in rituals is a critically important social obligation, as important as productive work in ensuring successful outcomes in agriculture as well as building a new house.[1]

Across the region, Buddhists, Muslims, Christians, Hindus, and animists are all part of related ritual systems, although they all differ in practitioner, context, meaning, and intention. Often they share common religious practices such as food offerings, pilgrimages, and the use of candles, flowers, and incense. Even individual food items may cross religions— hard-boiled eggs, coconuts, and limes all find their place in rituals in the region. Everyday rice can become a celebratory dish by the addition of turmeric, lemongrass, aromatic herbs, and garnishes of fried onions.

Celebratory meals, if they are not vegetarian, usually involve more meat than everyday meals—a buffalo sacrifice, boiled chickens, a pig's head. As in other parts of the world, items that are expensive or time consuming to make are featured on special occasions. In short, celebrations of all sorts revolve around food.

FEEDING THE SPIRITS

In Southeast Asia, many believe that humans share the world with spirits, unseen inhabitants who must be propitiated or appeased with food. Feeding spirits involves simple practices such as a nurse leaving a small serving of rice and fruit in a spirit house in the northeast corner of her Bangkok house on her way to work, as well as a mammoth community-wide feast of merit held in the uplands of Lao PDR or Vietnam, when a buffalo might be sacrificed. In the ancient Southeast Asian spirit of pluralism, people do not always reject earlier forms of ritual practices when they become Christian or Buddhist or Muslim, even though world religions discourage the pluralism that is often celebrated as tolerance in Southeast Asia. Thus, feeding spirits might be done by devout Buddhists or Christians in combination with their regular religious practices.

In the uplands, people give feasts to gain political and spiritual potency. Upland traditions include feasts of merit, where people compete for status

Spirit house guards crops on the banks of the Mekong River, 2002.

by sacrificing buffalo or pigs and providing rice meals to guests, who may re-
ciprocate directly by providing uncooked rice to the sponsors, or indirectly
through return feasts.[2] Ancestors receive offerings of food and rice beer and
in return confer blessings on household members, particularly when people
enter or leave the household through marriage or death. Fortunately, ancestors only eat the essence of the food, leaving the material food for their
descendents to enjoy communally. Spirits also guard spaces like kitchens,
house compounds, and village gates. Ancestors and guardian spirits may be
owed tribute in the form of the hind leg of an animal, for example.

The Hmong, who live primarily in the uplands of Thailand and Lao
PDR, include animal sacrifice in their ancestral feasts. Men ritually sacrifice animals such as pigs and chickens, which are then cleaned and cooked
by women and eaten by all family and guests. Men eat first and drink rice
or corn liquor at all rituals; women eat what is left and don't drink rice
liquor. At a Hmong wedding ritual in northern Thailand, the chicken was
boiled, the breasts and legs fed to elders, and the rest made into soup. The
bride's family gave the bride a pig that she gave to her new in-laws so that
everyone would eat well when the newly married couple arrived home. It
is noted that "meat is a prestige food, a sign of wealth; eating meat during
the marriage means that one will eat well for the rest of one's life."[3] Feasts
of merit occur among the Kachin and Chin of Burma as well. Ceremonies
and rituals transmitted through generations are often maintained in the
marginalized upland regions of mainland Southeast Asia among transna-
tional minorities such as the Dai, Hmong, and Akha. But upland peoples
and lowlanders exist in complex relations with one another, and have
for centuries. Uplanders often define themselves in relation to lowland
peoples, emphasizing who they are not—not literate, not civilized, not
Buddhist, for example.

Spirit practices coexist with the world religions, and are seamlessly integrated into ritual events. The Shan of Burma and Thailand, Theravada
Buddhists, offer rice to the ancestors before it is consumed by the living,
uniting the living and the dead in commensality and transforming the
food into ritual leftovers.[4] Thai guardian spirits receive a wide variety of
food offerings, and the type of food given offers clues as to whether that
spirit is considered benevolent or evil.[5]

Among the Burmese, who also practice Theravada Buddhism, nats are
a class of supernatural beings who can cause suffering or bring good for-
tune to people. And, like monks and people, they must be fed. The house
nat resides in a coconut hanging from the southeast pillar of the house.
Village nats reside in small shrines near the village gates and may be given
fruit and small bits of everyday food. Nature nats reside in trees, waterfalls,

forests, and rice fields, for example, while other nats reside in the heavens and protect Buddhism; these latter nats are offered only vegetarian food dishes. Bananas, coconuts, liquor, flowers, and money are common offerings. Some groups of people also have hereditary obligations to propitiate nats. When nats receive offerings of food, it is usually redistributed to the people attending the nat's festival. Small intimate ceremonies and large annual festivals take place at the nats' shrine, and most involve both ritual and commercial opportunities for people to eat together.[6]

RICE RITUALS

In some parts of Southeast Asia, rice is difficult to grow; in areas where it flourishes, it still needs constant attention from humans to thrive. Everywhere in Southeast Asia rice has a feminine soul that must be placated and carefully nurtured. Mother rice is the self-sacrificing mother who is given gifts and offerings of food to guarantee a bountiful rice harvest. She is treated like a pregnant woman whose every whim must be indulged. Known as *mae prasob* in Thai, and related terms in other Southeast Asian languages, she determines the auspicious days to plant, transplant, and harvest rice. *Dewi Sri*, the Hindu-Balinese goddess of rice, is similarly honored in Java, Bali, and Malaysia. Where rice is not the core starch, such as in Eastern Indonesia where it is difficult to grow, it is still the highest prestige food, and it is served at ceremonials and valued over other staples.[7]

The rice fields are protected by spirits who must be ritually fed to produce the highest yields. Transplanting in particular is marked by ritual; during transplanting in the rite of *Liang Phi Ta Hek* among the Lao, spirits of the rice fields are fed and honored with the following blessing:

I plant the rice shoot; may you be green as the Thao.

I plant the second shoot; may you be as green as the grass of the ninth month.

I plant the third shoot; may the gong of nine akm (measure of diameter) be mine.

I plant the fourth shoot; may the ninety thousand pounds of gold be mine.

I plant the fifth shoot; may ninety thousand baskets of rice be mine.

I plant the sixth shoot; may I have a wife to sleep by my side.

I plant the seventh shoot; may a rare elephant saddled in gold and silver be mine.

Glory! Prosperity![8]

Religious rituals are closely integrated with the seasonal agricultural cycle—primarily irrigated rice in mainland Southeast Asia. However, the adoption of high-yielding varieties of rice and other technologies that permit two or three crops a year alter the significance of Buddhist celebrations, since the cycle of planting, transplanting, and harvesting is no longer in sync with Buddhist seasonal rituals. This results in differences in the emphasis of rural and urban Buddhist rituals.

BUDDHISM

The predominant religious tradition in mainland Southeast Asia is Theravada Buddhism, a community-based religion practiced in varying intensities and styles in Burma, Thailand, Lao PDR, and Cambodia. There are also growing numbers of practitioners following other Buddhist traditions in Malaysia and Vietnam.

Buddhism and food intertwine at the level of rituals and lay offerings, but also at the level of ideology and text. Fasting and not feasting is the Buddhist pattern, recalling always the middle way, avoiding the extremes of asceticism. However, community-based rituals with lay participation are usually celebrated with elaborate shared meals.

Monks, like spirits, need to be fed. But the Buddhist pattern of moderate asceticism is reflected in the practice of restricting the number and timing of meals for monks. Monks fast from noon, accepting only tea or sweet

Lao Buddhist women present rice offerings to monks, 2002.

drinks in the afternoon and evening. Buddhists accrue merit through *dana* (meritorious giving), including giving daily food to monks. This is one route to a better rebirth and to avoiding dangers in the present life. Most of those feeding monks and spirits are women. In all the Theravada countries, women are the most generous supporters of temples, providing the food for early morning alms rounds, cooked dishes for the monks' noon meal, and uncooked rice for special ceremonies and community rituals at the temple. In a more commercial vein, women often sell food at temple fairs as a means of making merit (and money). For example, a complex snack—crispy stuffed Vietnamese pancakes (*kanom bueng yuan*)—was sold at aristocratic temple fairs in Bangkok for a high price in the reign of Rama 6 (1910–1925).[9] Still today, expensive or time-consuming special foods may only be available for sale at temple fairs in urban centers like Bangkok, Rangoon, or Phnom Penh.

Ordinations of new monks, giving gifts of robes to monks, and consecrations of religious buildings and Buddha images are all occasions for pilgrimages and festive meals. Food connects urban and rural communities on these occasions. Income differences may be apparent in the foods given to monks; however, any food given with a good intention is valued. Ethnic heritage may also be reflected in the food given to monks. For example, a rice-flour noodle known as *kanom jeen* mixed with a fish curry (*nam yaa plaa chon*) is often served at temple events in areas of Thailand where the Mon settled. It is made from snakehead fish, garlic, shallots, shrimp paste, galangal, and ginger, and served over coiled rice noodles.[10]

Youngest novice receives the last offerings of rice from Thai villagers.

After the food is given to monks, everyone who participated in the service shares the donated food. In Buddhist ceremonies, white thread is used to define sacred space and transfer the merit made by feeding monks and spirits to all who participated in the ritual. Merit made by feeding monks can also be transferred to ancestors in general or to recently deceased relatives through a ritual known as *kluat nam;* water that has been blessed by the monks is slowly poured into another container or into the ground, while monks chant appropriate Pali stanzas. Thus, both food and merit are widely shared with the living and the dead.

Theravada Buddhists are not generally vegetarian. In the Theravada tradition, meat dishes are given to monks in most communities. However, Theravada Buddhists have some problems with meat offerings. In Burma, for example, food offerings to the monks during the Lenten season (July–October) have no meat; women offer food "free from killing."[11] In Burma in particular, releasing domestic animals from slaughter accrues lots of merit. In Thailand, the release of birds or fish is more common.

In Buddhist communities, it is more often the elderly who fast, meditate, and keep extra precepts all day, because they no longer have to worry about the work of food production and preparation. Women and the elderly are also more likely to enter into longer-term vegetarian fasts. New Buddhist movements such as Santi Asoke require their adherents to be vegetarian. Recently, more Theravada Buddhists are taking on the Mahayana practice of fasting a few days a month.

In Mahayana traditions, vegetarian meals are more common among monks and laity. For example, vegetarian dishes are popular in Vietnam.

Lao refugees resettled in North America transfer merit to their deceased relatives.

Vegetarian Soup

This vegetarian soup is used for fasting for the new moon and full moon fasts, and for longer fasts. This tamarind-based soup could be modified and made with ground meat and meat stock instead of tofu and vegetable stock.

5 cups vegetable stock, water, or chicken stock

1 cup tamarind water (dissolve 1/4 cup tamarind pulp softened in 1 cup hot water; let sit; squeeze out pulp and seeds)

1 cup chopped pineapple

3 chopped tomatoes

2 cups okra (cut in half)

2 cups bean sprouts

1/2 cup tofu cut in small squares

1 tbsp sugar

1 tsp salt

1 tsp soy sauce

Bring water or stock and tamarind liquid to boil. Add okra and pineapple (and ground meat, if using) and boil for 3 minutes. Reduce heat, add tofu, tomatoes, sugar, bean sprouts, salt, and soy sauce and simmer for 2 minutes. Adjust seasonings, and serve with rice. Garnish with chopped coriander, minced chiles, and fried shallots.

Southeast Asian cuisines generally are not vegetarian. Meat and fish products are welcome additions to meals rich in vegetables. Vegetarians—local and visitors—usually seek out South Asian food vendors. Recently, specialty urban vegetarian restaurants have opened for tourists and locals where purely vegetarian dishes are available. However, market food dishes use small amounts of fish sauce, shrimp paste, or oyster sauce as basic ingredients. Even if a customer requests vegetables only—no meat—the dish rarely meets the exacting standards of western vegans or vegetarians.

MUSLIM CELEBRATIONS

Muslims are a minority in some parts of Thailand, Cambodia, Burma, and Vietnam, but a majority in Malaysia and Indonesia. Muslims are the only people in Southeast Asia who define themselves more by what they do not eat than by what they do eat. Pork avoidance is critically important to Muslim belief and practice. Thus, food in Muslim households and communities becomes a means of defining identity. Muslims in Southeast Asia are the people whose kitchens are pure, in contrast to the surrounding kitchens that are full of pig products. This is particularly important in Southeast Asia, where pig products are so well established in both the local cuisines and the restaurants established by Chinese immigrants.

Muslims are not vegetarian, but they do have special rules surrounding food. Halal is an Arabic word meaning lawful or allowed. Halal rules determine how animals are butchered, for example, and specify prayers that render the food acceptable. Rules also forbid the consumption of blood or alcohol. In the seven months pregnancy ritual celebrated in East Javanese villages, the sacrificial animal is killed according to Islamic rules, including reciting a short Islamic prayer while collecting the blood. But the villagers' interpretation is essentially pre-Islamic; the blood is offered to the indigenous spirits of the land.[12]

Throughout Southeast Asia, there is variation in how Islam is practiced, as it is integrated into systems of *adat* or customary law. Southeast Asian Muslims have generally been more concerned with rituals than doctrinal Islam; however, that situation is rapidly changing in the face of recent Islamic reforms.[13] Muslim groups in Malaysia and Indonesia selectively interpret and integrate elements of Islamic practice. For example, the Arabic term *muhrim* refers to close family members who may not marry one another. Malay Muslims in Sumatra include more people in this category, including adopted relatives.[14]

Slametan (communal meals) are an important part of Muslim ceremonies, particularly in Central Java. More rarely, they may be used to mark Christian celebrations as well. These feasts, called *kenduri* in Malay, are held to mark most calendar rituals, house construction, and life-cycle events including weddings, funerals, and journeys— particularly pilgrimages to Mecca. Slametan feasts often involve casual last-minute invitations to male household representatives, and usually include a formal redistribution of food. Neighboring households bring trays of cooked rice, accompanying dishes, and snacks, and after formal speeches and prayers, the food is redivided onto individual trays or plates and given to all men present, who take their supply of food home to share with their families. This is less a communal feast than a ritualized take-out with essentially the same food exchanged among households.[15]

Ramadan, a special period of fasting and prayer for Muslims, falls in the ninth lunar month of the Islamic calendar. It is a stricter fast than the Buddhist fasts described above because it is not voluntary, but a requirement for all observant Muslims. The purpose of the fast is to strive for physical and spiritual purification. No food or water is consumed between dawn and dusk; during the fasting period, people try to refrain from using angry language, smoking cigarettes, and indulging in sexual activity. There are dispensations for pregnant women, the sick, and children, but it is the elderly who find the fast particularly difficult.

Collective fasting is also a time for collective eating. Among the Minangkabau of Sumatra, reciprocal sharing occurs as special meals are exchanged with kin two days before the fast begins. Muslims also give food and alms to the poor at the end of Ramadan. It is customary to give gifts of unhulled rice to poor villagers; rice is collected at the local mosque and redistributed to poorer members of the community. Breaking the fast usually begins with drinking water and eating dates. Malay Muslims may enjoy a sherbet of milk, rose water, and other special sweets of palm sugar and coconut. A new feature among the middle and upper classes in urban Malaysia is breaking the fast in elegant hotels. Critics have pointed out that exorbitant hotel buffets break the spirit of Ramadan.

Hari Raya, marking the end of the fasting month, is like a public festival in Malaysia and Indonesia. In Java, at the end of the fasting period, lower-status persons beg higher-status persons for forgiveness for any possible injuries over the past year. In the days after Hari Raya, Minangkabau women of the same lineage share a meal and take gifts of hulled rice and cakes to their husband's relatives and receive a meal of cooked rice and *sambal* in return. These and other food exchanges at the end of the fasting month strengthen the alliances between lineages.[16] The end of the fasting month is a time for reconciliation and forgiveness, as well as an occasion to display new clothes and fine foods. Indonesians refer to the celebration that ends the fasting month as *lebaran;* it entails the communal consumption of delicious food among the living and deceased ancestors. Islamic reformists remind the community that it is spiritual food in the form of prayers and verses from the Koran that their deceased relatives need, not human food.[17]

One of the popular celebratory dishes for Malaysians and Indonesians is the time-consuming but delicious stew known as *rendang.* The Minangkabau people of West Sumatra are justly famous for their cuisine, known as *nasi Padang* (Padang rice). Perhaps best known is the labor-intensive beef rendang, a mixture of beef, coconut, ginger, and spices slowly braised until it is almost dried; in this form, it is suitable for use while traveling. There are many good recipes all with regional variation.

Beef Rendang

This is a typical rendition.

Flavor Paste

1 nutmeg
5 cloves
6 shallots, coarsely chopped
3 cloves garlic, coarsely chopped
fresh hot chiles, coarsely chopped (adjust to taste)
2 inches fresh turmeric, coarsely chopped
2 inches fresh ginger, coarsely chopped
2 inches fresh galangal, sliced against the grain

2 lbs stewing beef or other well-marbled beef cut in 2-inch cubes.
2 1/2 cups unsweetened coconut milk
3 stalks lemongrass, cut in 2-inch pieces and crushed
1 cinnamon stick
7 wild lime leaves
1 tsp salt

Grind the nutmeg and cloves into a coarse powder. Add shallots, garlic, chiles, turmeric, ginger, and galangal, and pulse to a chunky paste consistency. In a wide shallow cooking pot or skillet (ideally nonstick), mix the beef and the flavor paste. Add the coconut milk, lemongrass, wild lime leaves, and salt. Stir well and bring to a gentle boil over medium heat. Reduce heat and simmer uncovered at a slow bubble, stirring often to prevent sticking. Continue simmering until the liquid has almost disappeared, around 2 hours. When the liquid has evaporated, allow the beef to brown slowly, stirring to prevent sticking. Garnish with chopped wild lime leaves.

CHRISTIAN CELEBRATION

Christians are a religious minority in Southeast Asia, except in the Philippines, where the Christian majority celebrate all the ritual events of the Christian calendar. The special Christmas Eve meal may include ham, stuffed poultry, and sweets.[18] Christmas is not an official holiday elsewhere. In the Philippines, many foods used to mark both personal and seasonal rituals are derived from Spanish dishes (including rellenos, stuffed foods) and are considered fiesta fare. Christmas is a new occasion for festive eating among non-Christians. Urban shopping malls in

Singapore, Bangkok, and other cities display Christmas decorations and festive seasonal fruitcakes along with other sweets.

CELEBRATING THE NEW YEAR

Every country in Southeast Asia celebrates the coming of the new year, regardless of the varying dates of the event. For each location, there are unique customs and special foods to celebrate the occasion. The celebration in Vietnam is perhaps the best known. Tet Nguyen Dan (often referred to as Tet), the Vietnamese New Year falling between mid-January to mid-February, is the most important celebration in the country; at the same time, it celebrates being Vietnamese. At Tet, offerings must be given to deities and family members must return home to honor the ancestors together. In preparation, families clean, decorate, cook, and shop for festive specialties like candies and special cakes. Vietnamese celebrate Tet by literally "eating the lunar New Year."

Glutinous rice dishes are particularly significant during Tet. They are most prominent in the form of special rice cakes wrapped in banana leaves and boiled. These are always prepared in advance to celebrate Tet. Rice cakes appear on every ancestor altar and are consumed at every New Year's meal, first fresh, and later fried. North, central, and south celebrate with different dishes, but all feast to guarantee success and prosperity in the coming year. Other special foods from Hoi An, Central Vietnam include candied kumquats, a very sweet and labor intensive item to prepare; fatty pork pickled in fish sauce; special sausages; and a number of preserved vegetable dishes such as pickled onions and green rice cakes.[19] Cambodian New Year also features special rice cakes made of glutinous rice and bananas. These are somewhat easier to make than the Vietnamese rice cakes.

Glutinous Rice Cakes

1 cup soaked glutinous rice

1 cup coconut milk

pinch of salt

bananas cut in 2-inch lengths

Steam glutinous rice, adding a sprinkle of coconut milk every 5 minutes. Mix with fork to distribute evenly. Place about a quarter of a cup of cooked rice on a square of banana leaf. Place a piece of banana on the rice, roll rice up to cover banana, and roll up in the banana leaf into a cylindrical roll, tucking the side edges under the roll. In the Cambodian version, place in a steamer and steam for about 25 minutes; in the Malay version, grill for about 10 minutes, turning once. Slice and serve with sauces.

A Burmese Buddhist form of giving at the New Year involves feeding whoever comes from the four directions, regardless of whether they are known to the person preparing the food. This kind of giving, or *dana*, encourages benevolence and detachment.[20]

RITES OF PASSAGE

Marriages, births, ordinations, and funerals mark transitions in the life cycle. In the past, topknot cutting and ear piercing were also occasions for celebrations. The foods served depend on the local religious tradition. In some communities, such as the Minangkabau of Sumatra, many dishes cooked for life-cycle rituals are not eaten outside these contexts.[21] A special rice cake is used in the betrothal ceremony in Hue, central Vietnam. It is stuffed with green peas and coconut and served in tiny square leaf boxes.

Contrasts in economic status between families are most visible in life-cycle rituals. For example, a young girl's ear-piercing ceremony in Burma might be accompanied by a meal of four fish and four meat dishes, plus a vegetable dish, soup, and rice in a wealthy family, and pickled mangoes, pea curry, and salted fish with rice in a poor family.[22]

Throughout Southeast Asia, in addition to the simplest plate of raw or lightly steamed vegetables, there are complex vegetable salads that can be served as appetizers, snacks, or accompaniments to rice meals. These dishes, known as *kerabu* in Malaysia, *yam* in Thailand, and *gado-gado* in Indonesia, make use of whatever vegetables are available in market or garden, served with a spicy dressing. Because they are time consuming to prepare, there are palace versions of these dishes. *Urap* is a Javanese court dish and is considered an essential part of ritual meals celebrating birthdays or other special events. The Thai also have a special salad that is considered the royal way to honor monks. Called *yam tawai*, literally salad for honoring monks, it was presented to monks on the inauguration of the Temple of the Emerald Buddha in Bangkok in 1809.[23]

Celebratory Salad

This salad is a synthesis of several Southeast Asian celebratory salads, adapted to readily available Euro-American ingredients.

1 cup bean sprouts
1 cup green beans cut into 1-inch pieces

1 1/2 cups shredded cabbage

1 cup thinly sliced cucumbers

1 coarsely grated carrot

(optional) 1 large chicken breast, poached and shredded

1 cup shredded jackfruit or pineapple

mint, watercress, and basil leaves to garnish

Dressing

1/4 cup tamarind water

1 tbsp fish sauce

2 tbsp brown sugar

2 cloves garlic

2 shallots

2 chiles

1 can coconut milk

Grind garlic, shallots, and chiles together. Heat gently with coconut milk and blend in remainder of dressing ingredients. Blanch bean sprouts in boiling water for 10 seconds and rinse with cool water. Blanch green beans in the same water for about 2 minutes and rinse with cool water. Blanch cabbage in the same water for about 1 minute and rinse with cool water. Add cucumbers, carrots, shredded chicken, and fruit when the blanched vegetables are cool. Add dressing just before serving. Garnish with coriander leaves, fried shallots, roasted grated coconut, sesame seeds, and chopped peanuts.

As in other food cultures of the world, personal recipes passed down in families are often brought out to celebrate special occasions.

NOTES

1. Anthony Reid, *Southeast Asia in the Age of Commerce (1450–1680)*. Vol. 1, *The Land below the Winds* (New Haven, CT: Yale University Press, 1988), p. 171.

2. Cornelia Kammerer and Nicola Tannenbaum explore the relation between upland feasts of merit and Buddhist merit-making activities in their edited volume, *Merit and Blessing in Mainland Southeast Asia in Comparative Perspective*, monograph 45, Yale Southeast Asia Studies (1996). They argue that there are also upland groups whose feasting does not confer status, but rather blessings.

3. P. Symonds, *Calling the Soul in a Hmong Village* (Seattle: University of Washington Press, 2004), p. 69.

4. Ing-Britt Trankell, "Cooking, Care, and Domestication: A Culinary Ethnography of the Tai Yong, Northern Thailand," *Uppsala Studies in Cultural Anthropology* 21 (1995): 134.

5. These offerings to guardian spirits help people address Buddhist paradox in a very concrete way, particularly women who prepare food offerings but who have fewer opportunities to make merit by becoming religious specialists. The most valued roles are closed to most women. Recently, however, Thai women have claimed ordination as female monks rather than the less-valued women's role as "nun." See Penny Van Esterik, "Feeding Their Faith: Recipe Knowledge among Thai Buddhist Women," *Food and Foodways* 1, no. 1:198–215. See also my third chapter in *Materializing Thailand* (Oxford: Berg Press, 2000), where I discuss Buddhism and gender.

6. Materials on nat worship come from Melford Spiro, *Burmese Supernaturalism* (Englewood Cliffs, NJ: Prentice-Hall, 1967).

7. Monica Janowski, introduction to *Kinship and Food in South East Asia*, ed. Monica Janowski and F. Kerlogue (Copenhagen: NIAS Press, 2007), p. 17.

8. Harry Benda and John Larkin, *The World of Southeast Asia: Selected Historical Readings* (New York: Harper and Row, 1967), p. 302. There are many other references to rituals of rice planting for individual countries in Southeast Asia.

9. Thanes Wongyannava, "Chinese Restaurants in Bangkok," in *The Transformation of Chinese Haute Cuisine in Bangkok's Chinese Restaurants* (research report, Toyoto Foundation, 2000), p. 16.

10. Kanit Muntarbhorn argues that this dish is Mon in origin, *Gastronomy in Asia*, bk. 1 (Bangkok: M. T. Press, 2007), p. 85.

11. Naoko Kumada, "In the World of Rebirth: Politics, Economy, and Society of Burmese Buddhists" (unpublished PhD dissertation, 2001), p. 63

12. R. Heringe, "Reconstructing the Whole: Seven Months Pregnancy Ritual in Kerek, East Java," in *Kinship and Food*, ed. Janowski and Kerlogue, p. 39.

13. For example, Malays could be prosecuted for eating in public during Ramadan. Malays who used to eat in Chinese, Indian, or fusion restaurants are more attentive now to eat only in restaurants marked as halal. See also the case studies in *Kinship and Food*, ed. Janowski and Kerlogue.

14. F. Kerlogue, "Food and the Family: Assimilation in a Malay Village," in *Kinship and Food*, ed. Janowski and Kerlogue, p. 57.

15. John Pemberton, *On the Subject of Java* (Ithaca: Cornell University Press, 1994), pp. 244–46.

16. C. Davis, "Food, Fertility, and Kinship in Minangkabau," in *Kinship and Food*, ed. Janowski and Kerlogue, p. 82.

17. K. Telle, "Nurturance and the Spectre of Neglect: Sasak Ways of Dealing with the Dead," in *Kinship and Food*, ed. Janowski and Kerlogue, p. 142.

18. Amy Besa and Rory Dorotan, *Memories of Philippine Kitchens* (New York: Steward, Tabori, and Chang, 2006), p. 13. Many upland groups such as the Karen

have been Christian for a long time. Vietnamese Catholics celebrate with their own special foods.

19. Nir Avieli, "Vietnamese New Year Rice Cakes: Iconic Restive Dishes and Contested National Identity," *Ethnology* 44, no. 2 (2005).

20. Kumada, *In the World of Rebirth*, p. 117.

21. Lisa Heldke argues that this is a problem when outsiders demand access to specialty foods only used for ritual occasions. See *Exotic Appetites* (New York: Routledge, 2003).

22. Aung Aung Taik, *Under the Golden Pagoda: The Best of Burmese Cooking* (San Francisco: Chronicle Books, 1993), p. 10.

23. David Thompson, *Thai Food* (Berkeley, CA: Ten Speed Press, 2002), p. 374.

7

Diet and Health

How does diet contribute to maintaining and restoring health in Southeast Asia? This chapter examines some of the ideologies underlying the relation between food and disease, particularly the humoral system, and then considers the nutritional challenges related to recent changes in local food systems.

Western biomedicine entered Southeast Asia with colonial missionaries, but its reception was mixed. Often the royal families in Burma, Thailand, and Cambodia accepted new surgical techniques or vaccinations, for example, encouraging some use of biomedicine by national elites in the late 1800s. The Dutch introduced European medicine to Indonesia much earlier, in the 1600s. At that time, there was little to choose from between European and Javanese herbal medicine, and in fact there was good potential for an interchange between Dutch and Javanese herbal therapies.[1]

Although biomedicine predominates throughout Southeast Asia today, it coexists with indigenous approaches to health and healing. All countries in the region have strong traditions of herbal medicine and massage or manipulation; in addition, people self-medicate with both allopathic and indigenous medicines. Most methods of healing include dietary directives.

Today Thailand, Malaysia, and Singapore offer tourists the opportunity for medical tourism, and provide internationally recognized biomedical services, often lodged in luxurious spas, where treatments are combined with meals designed to enhance healing. Yet tourist appeal is enhanced by the availability of local healing practices such as traditional massage, herbal medicines, herbal saunas, and meditation. The integration of bio-medicine and traditional healing practices is not just for tourists; holistic healing is coming back full circle as the world seeks a healthy balance between medical interventions and lifestyle changes.

HUMORAL SYSTEMS AND HEALING FOODS

Many local health systems based on food and diet can be linked back to humoral systems. Humoral systems stressing the hot/cold contrast probably traveled from India to Arabia, Greece, and Europe, and could have entered Southeast Asia influenced by several of these distinct but related humoral systems of medicine. Ayurvedic medicine—an ancient Indian healing system that links, body, temperment, and food—is probably the best known humoral system in Asia. Medical systems in Malaysia and Indonesia show the strongest influence of Islamic medicine, while Vietnam practices a variant of Chinese medicine. In general, humoral systems view humans as having a unique constitution composed of earth, fire, water, and wind. Humans' constitutions can be altered by diet when necessary. In Southeast Asia, the wind element tends to be stressed, as in diseases related to *lom* in Thailand and *angin* in Malaysia. Blood, a hot humor, and phlegm, a cold humor, need to be kept in balance; illnesses and reproductive states upset the humoral balance and require special dietary attention.[2] The logic of the humoral system lingers in North America, in expressions like "feed a cold; starve a fever" and "cool as a cucumber."

The Indianized states of Southeast Asia likely included Ayurvedic medical practitioners in their courts. Thai traditional medicine borrowed from Ayurvedic medicine and combined it with an indigenous system probably widespread throughout the region, particularly in Lao PDR and Cambodia. It is difficult to confirm to what extent Thai traditional medicine is derived from Ayurvedic sources, since most classical texts were destroyed in the Burmese wars in the 1760s. The earliest historical evidence for Thai traditional medicine comes from the medical texts of King Narai (1657–1688) and is primarily a listing of herbal prescriptions.

Medical texts were considered royal texts, the property of the palace, but they have been made available to the people in different and often incomplete forms over the last century. For example, the classical texts of Thai traditional medicine are inscribed in Pali and Khmer on the walls of Wat Pho, a temple located behind the Grand Palace in Bangkok. Inscriptions on the temple walls include texts and anatomical drawings to guide contemporary students. Here traditional practitioners are still taught the ancient arts of massage and pharmacology. Thai traditional doctors must qualify as pharmacists before they can study medicine.[3] Both texts and practical knowledge of the healing arts must be directly passed down from teacher to pupil and require the ritual honoring of the teacher before healing can occur. This is known in Thai as *wai khru*.

Southeast Asia imported from India some ideas about the cooling and heating properties of food and how food affects individuals at certain stages of their life cycle in certain seasons. This exchange of knowledge probably took place during the process of Indianization. But since the region did not import the South Asian system of castes and subcastes, the heating and cooling properties of food and people had no connotation of purity and pollution. Thus in most Southeast Asian communities there was in no need to separate food preparation and consumption by groups; everyone could eat together.[4]

Healers

Midwives, specialists in traditional massage, herbalists, monks who heal, Muslim mystics, and shamans all contribute their expertise to the varied healing strategies in the region. Spirit doctors and shamans practice in some minority communities and bring their unique healing techniques with them as immigrants and refugees to other parts of the world. When the Hmong from the uplands of Lao PDR entered North America as refugees, the clash between biomedical and shamanistic healing became painfully visible. A young Hmong girl in California was diagnosed with epilepsy. To her family, her symptoms suggested she might be a shaman, and they sought the spiritual origins of her disease and offered animal sacrifices and herbal medications. Who can say whether her disease was caused by soul loss or aberrant brain cells? Shamanistic rituals helped the family cope with a devastating illness.[5]

In the Theravada Buddhist communities of Southeast Asia, some monks, particularly forest monks who reside alone and practice meditation, gain reputations for their skills in healing through herbal and spiritual methods. In the past, when villagers might not have had access to any health services, monks were honored as valuable healers who helped reduce suffering out of loving kindness, free of charge. Ritual speech—words spoken over medicinal mixtures—can be called upon in cures. Whether efficacy can be attributed to the placebo effect or the peace of mind that comes from practicing morality is not of great concern, particularly in households where no other remedies are available. Spiritual healing is particularly important in palliative care, treating chronic diseases, and when illnesses have a mental health component. When Cambodians fled their country as refugees, escaping war and the repressive regime of the Khmer Rouge, healers known as Khru Khmer offered a variety of traditional medical services, including massage and herbal therapies, in the refugee camps.

FOOD AS MEDICINE: MEDICINE AS FOOD

Food and health are intimately linked in Southeast Asia. Regional variation in food practices is reflected in the distribution of diseases. Different diets encourage different diseases, even within the same country. Indian Malaysians suffer more from diabetes than Chinese Malaysians, who suffer more from throat cancer. Yet in every country in Southeast Asia, emphasis is also on foods that heal—well-balanced food dishes and meals, not simply medicinal foods. The therapeutic use of foods and pharmaceuticals is determined by their taste. Foods are generally classified as hot, sour, salty, or sweet, with pharmaceutical use requiring an expansion of the taste variants of foods to nine, including fragrant, toxic, and bland. Foods are combined in dishes and meals to maintain balance and create healing contrasts.[6]

Much of the research on the heating and cooling properties of foods consists of lists of foods and their classifications. But these are dynamic systems based on personal experience, season of the year, and life stage, and not usefully reduced to standardized lists. Nevertheless, there is some consistency in the region concerning the classification of foods; for example, papaya is a heating fruit while most fruits and vegetables, particularly juicy ones, are cold. Sour fruits are particularly cold. Okra and squashes are cooling, but bitter vegetables (and medicines) are hot. Fats are hot, as are animal meats and salted fish. Rice, like most starchy staples, is neutral, as is fresh fish—the dietary staples in most of Southeast Asia.

Most people in good health ignore humoral considerations until they are sick or pregnant. But in Malaysia and Indonesia, humoral logic requires a man and a woman to be in a cool state in order to conceive a child. Following childbirth, the woman remains in a dangerous cold state, and must be ritually and practically heated up with heating foods and medicines.[7] Illnesses are also classified as hot or cold; fevers are hot; rheumatism is cold. In countries where pharmacists advise on treatment and provide western or herbal drugs without prescriptions, self-medication is very common. Generally, traditional medicines are not considered as hot as biomedical allopathic medicines such as antibiotics.

Herbal medicines are part of health maintenance systems, not simply treatments for specific diseases. They can be taken in alcohol, water, or rice water; swallowed in pill form; or rubbed on the body. In Lao PDR, communities are even more dependent on traditional herbal medicines, since few people outside of cities have access to primary health care. Herbal mixtures are taken orally, applied to body parts, or used for a steam "sauna." These herbal saunas are particularly popular with women. Most striking are the number of products used in each concoction; common ingredients include chiles, red ginger, sesame oil, cotton seed, opium, bark, leaves, roots, and ground snail shells. One healer in Lao PDR who wrote out his list of mixtures knew cures for goiters, ear infections, epilepsy, beriberi, food poisoning, weakness of pregnancy or recovery after birth, coughs, infected wounds, fever, shock, cramps, heart palpitations, skin abscesses, headaches, hernias, constipation, and diarrhea.[8]

Because of the rich biodiversity of Lao PDR, the ethnic diversity of its peoples, and the scarcity of health practitioners and products, the country makes good use of its herbal resources; it is also attracting bioprospectors from pharmaceutical companies based in industrial countries. The Research Institute of Medicinal Plants in Lao PDR has permitted collectors to seek out plants and information from traditional healers for the

Hmong women bring in wild forest foods and medicinal products to sell in the morning market, Vientiane, 2002.

purpose of developing new drugs to combat malaria, cancer, HIV/AIDS, and diseases of the central nervous system. The active components in some of the plants they have found have been patented by the University of Illinois and delivered to Glaxo-SmithKline, a British pharmaceutical company, for further development. In the future, perhaps 1% of the profits could make their way back to Laos in some form.[9]

Another well-known herbal medicine system thrives in Java. Here, traditional tonics known as *jamu* coexist with allopathic pharmaceuticals as a parallel system, rather than as replacements. *Jamu* and more recently gelatin capsules of dried *jamu* can be used to enhance health. Unlike traditional herbal mixtures on the mainland, *jamu* has been successfully commercialized and crosses all classes. *Jamu* can be used to increase breast milk, male potency, and appetite. Other mixtures enhance women's beauty and fitness, particular after childbirth. *Jamu* peddlers carry bottles of their own mixtures, but also mix tonics to meet the specific needs of their customers. As in other traditions in Southeast Asia, many of the ingredients are also used for cooking—ginger, turmeric, tamarind, and chiles are used in *jamu*, in addition to specifically medicinal herbs. While commercial *jamu* products are designed mostly for women, *jamu* also address specific health problems such as coughs, jaundice, or ulcers.[10]

The need for integrating medicinal tastes with individual constitutions is consistent with Ayurvedic medicine, Islamic medicine, and Chinese medicine. Although the links to Ayurvedic medicine, for example, are seldom made explicit outside of the study of esoteric medical texts, traces exist in the way people in Southeast Asian communities tend to individualize and personalize their foods and meals. For example, the food manager for Thailand's national football team explains how she prepares healthy food in accordance with each person's individual preferences, combined with the nature and requirements of the sport.[11]

NUTRITIONAL CHALLENGES

Most people in Southeast Asia can meet their basic food requirements, particularly for calories. All countries in the region show an improvement in food supply over the last few decades, primarily through increasing rice production by extending the amount of land under production and increasing the yield per area unit. Only Brunei and Singapore depend almost entirely on imported food.

International aid in the region has been actively involved with poverty-reduction programs including rural development, sustainable agricultural growth, and effective natural resource management. Yet these strategies often bypass the poorest of the poor—often minority groups in remote mountainous regions.[12] These regions are also facing environmental degradation resulting in losses of biodiversity; this is particularly important for groups relying on wild forest foods in their meals. Resource extraction from logging or mining, for example, also takes a toll on local food resources.

Not all communities and households in the region are food secure. In some marginalized regions, there are intergenerational cycles of poverty that are quite resistant to change. War disrupts food security as well as the lives of millions of people. Wars of national liberation, wars to "contain communism," and wars for local autonomy have all left scars, including the experience of hunger.

Food Insecurity and Hunger

The most food insecure countries are Burma, Cambodia, and Lao PDR. As a result, malnutrition rates are higher in those countries. Insufficient food consumption, in addition to infection and poor health, is the primary cause of malnutrition. Poor diets can also contribute to other problems such as iron deficiency, vitamin A deficiency resulting in night blindness, and iodine deficiency resulting in goiter, for example. In 1998, there was a 14.9 prevalence rate of iodine deficiency disorders in Southeast Asia, and millions of underweight children.[13]

In 2007, Lao PDR released a new report on food insecurity in the country, showing that 17% of urban and 25% of rural people are undernourished. The Lao PDR government, along with UN partners, is working towards reducing the infant mortality rate (62/1,000 in 2005), the under-five mortality rate (79/1,000 in 2005), and maternal mortality rate and malnutrition. The national prevalence of critical food poverty was around 18%, indicating that nearly one in five people did not have enough income to buy the food necessary to meet their daily minimum energy requirement of 1,638 calories. The upland peoples depend more on natural resources than food purchase, but their wild food sources are increasingly threatened. Rice contributed to more than 70% of calories consumed.[14] However, the overemphasis on increasing rice production suggests that food sufficiency is equated with rice sufficiency, a policy position that ignores the complexity of food systems and cuisines in the country, particularly in the uplands.[15]

Cambodia faces problems similar to those in Lao PDR, with many communities and households eating less than the minimal calories recommended. And like Lao PDR, most of those calories come from rice. The infant mortality rate of 98 deaths per 1,000 live births is dropping, as is the under-five mortality rate (143/1,000). But malnutrition remains a significant problem in the country. International assistance has focused on immunizations, food supplements in schools, and vitamin A supplementation. In 2005, only 14% of households used iodized salt.

The extent of malnutrition in Burma is harder to estimate. Burma produced enough rice to increase its exports in 2007. However, the UN World Food Program (WFP) argues that the military government's tight control over the movement of food and people is keeping an estimated five million Burmese without adequate nutrition. The WFP is concerned that the locally grown rice they purchase in the fertile delta region has to be entrusted to the expensive, corrupt government transportation system for distribution to food-insecure, remote communities.[16]

In the past, Burma's population has suffered high rates of anemia and goiter. There are active programs to achieve universal salt iodization and vitamin A supplementation in the country. However, armed conflict has increased the disparities between different parts of the country, leaving groups like the Shan, Kachin, and Karen without even the most basic health services. In 2005, the under-five mortality rate was 105/1,000, and the infant mortality rate was 75/1,000, according to UNICEF. These conditions were exacerbated and made more visible after cyclone Nargis in May 2008. The military government delayed or confiscated critically needed emergency supplies of food to victims of the cyclone, particularly the minority peoples.

In Vietnam, adult literacy rates are relatively high (men 94%, women 87%). The under-five mortality rate has dropped from 53/1,000 in 1990 to 19/1,000 in 2005. The infant mortality rate has dropped from 38/1,000 in 1990 to 16/1,000 in 2005. But UNICEF estimates that over 30% of children under five still suffer from some form of malnutrition. Vietnam has made extraordinary progress since the end of the American war; 96% of children are sleeping under mosquito nets, 83% of households consume iodized salt, and vitamin A supplementation is estimated at 95%.

Vietnam remains one of the 30 poorest countries in the world, in spite of these dramatic postwar improvements. The northern uplands remain particularly poor, partly due to isolation and the complexity of the ethnic diversity in the region. However, it is not the case that ethnic minority farmers are resistant to change for cultural reasons, but rather that they have poor access to resources and markets. They have readily adopted new crops such as lychee, tea, plums, and apricots, and have intensified rice production.[17]

Indonesia's children are still affected by the 2004 tsunami that killed 150,000 people in the country. Safe drinking water and malaria remain serious problems. The under-five mortality rate dropped to 36/1,000 in

2005 and infant mortality rates to 28/1,000. But 28% of children under five are still malnourished. Widespread growth-monitoring programs recorded that the percentage of underweight children decreased from 37.7 in 1992 to 28.5 in 1999, with disparities among social and economic groups narrowing over time.[18]

Many rice consumers are currently concerned about the growing food crisis caused by the soaring price of rice. In spring 2008, rice prices almost doubled on the international markets. Droughts, floods, and tropical storms are exacerbating food problems in the region, fueling fears of civil unrest, as the rice-dependent countries of Southeast Asia face rice shortages and high food prices. Many more communities may become food insecure in the future.

Food Secure Countries and the "Double Burden"

There is much optimism about food and nutrition in Southeast Asia. An important international food policy agency, IFPRI, identifies Southeast Asia as an area where there will be the most dramatic improvements in child nutrition by 2020. Intensive community-level nutrition programs in Thailand, the Philippines, and Malaysia have produced declines in maternal mortality and infant and child undernutrition. The improvement in nutritional status for mothers and children is no doubt related to the relatively high status of women in Southeast Asia compared to women in south and east Asia. As discussed in the Introduction, kinship systems that do not require women to leave their relatives when they marry, women's inheritance of land, and women's active role in food production all contribute to women's capacity to control their own food intake and that of their families. The region generally has less son preference compared to other parts of Asia, and girls and boys are fed similarly.

Food security and good health care systems in Thailand and Malaysia are reflected in the low infant and under-five mortality rates for both countries in 2005: 18/1,000 and 21/1,000 in Thailand, 10/1,000 and 12/1,000 in Malaysia. In the Philippines, the under-five mortality rate dropped from 62/1,000 in 1990 to 33/1,000 in 2005, and the infant mortality rate dropped from 41/1,000 to 25/1,000.

Food secure countries in Southeast Asia face a different set of problems, as their policy makers must deal with conditions related to both under- and overnutrition. This double dilemma is a result of improvements in food supply combined with changes in food habits. For example, although Thailand has low rates of malnutrition, some families may still have to deal with both low-birth-weight infants and overweight school children. In addition to an estimate of 9% low-birth-weight infants and 10–15% overweight children in primary schools in the country, about half the people in central Thailand and urban areas now have high cholesterol rates.[19]

A related challenge concerns the complex interactions between malnutrition and HIV/AIDS. There are more than 4 million people living with HIV/AIDS in Southeast Asia. Weight loss and malnutrition increases the risk of infection, and people living with HIV in the region identified food as their most immediate and critical need. In addition, anti-retroviral therapy only works effectively on people who are well nourished.[20]

Infant Feeding

Feeding infants and young children is a challenge for families worldwide. In Southeast Asia, infant feeding presents special challenges linked to colonial pasts and high labor-participation rates for women—in addition to conditions created by dietary globalization. In the region, as in the rest of the world until recently, infants who were breastfed usually thrived, while those who were fed artificially usually died. This is reflected in the aforementioned infant mortality rates. In rural communities, continued breastfeeding for to 2–3 years protected infants from malnutrition. However, breastfeeding was rarely exclusive, and the preference for very early introduction of rice gruels, for example, restricted the protein available from breastfeeding and introduced the potential for contamination. In areas where glutinous rice was the household staple, mothers often pre-chewed a wad of roasted glutinous rice for their infants. Public health officials from the 1940s to the present considered this practice as a marker of uncivilized behavior that needed to be eradicated. However, it was probably a better solution than colonial health officers realized, considering the few available options.

Until the last few decades, dairy products were rare in Southeast Asia, traditionally a nondairying region. Thus, there are great dietary contrasts between the milk-loving cultures of South Asia and the milk-hating cultures of East and Southeast Asia. In the nondairying regions of the humid tropics of Asia, large proportions of the population are lactose intolerant (unable to digest milk sugars without digestive upset). Some upland groups made use of buffalo milk, but milk and cheese are not common ingredients in the region. Products like canned sweetened condensed milk, and more recently, yogurt drinks, were more readily accepted in the region because they are more easily digested.

Colonial trade brought the early import of canned sweetened condensed milk, first to Indonesia (1875), later to Malaysia and Singapore, and from there spread throughout the region. Sweetened condensed milk is ideal for long-distance trade, as the high sugar content keeps it relatively unadulterated, even in the tropical heat. Imported first for the use of the European colonists, the product spread to the local elite and then throughout the population as the price of a small tin decreased. The skimmed-milk version of the product was particularly cheap. In addition, milk kitchens set up by the Dutch in the towns and cities of Indonesia provided sweetened condensed milk for infants who did not receive mothers' milk. Around 1910, Nestle's sales network was marketing the product in Javanese villages.[21] Breastfeeding support programs still encounter the problem of promotion of unsuitable baby foods.

Because milk did not fit into local Southeast Asian diets, these new products from Australia and Europe were adopted for special purposes such as infant feeding (with disastrous consequences), desserts like ice cream, and in coffee, tea, and tonic drinks like Ovaltine. UHT (ultra high temperature treatment) milk was introduced to the region in the 1970s and 1980s and has become very popular with children, along with yogurt drinks.

Food Safety

Eating is a dangerous activity. Fears about food safety are deeply rooted in Southeast Asia—indigenous fears made modern by recent scares about mad cow disease, SARS, and bird flu.[22] Reports of tofu full of arsenic, fake soy sauce with inappropriate additives, and formaldehyde in noodles joined persistent concerns about the dangers of using MSG, a popular additive throughout the area.

Indigenous concepts of spirit attacks and witchcraft included threats of the malevolent use of food—excrement made to look like a beef curry, fingernail clippings incorporated into a vegetable dish, and other examples of matter out of place. Food tasters protected royalty. Protection for ordinary people included feeding small amounts of food on miniature dishes to malevolent and protective spirits residing in spirit houses.

In the midst of rapid urbanization and modernization, street foods came under particular attack and were blamed for more than their share of health problems. Thus, freshly made foods sold on the street were assumed to be more dangerous to health than processed foods sold in supermarkets. But a recent study in Bangkok suggests that the situation is much more complex. Yeast doughnuts purchased from a food vendor are likely a higher risk for trans fats than those purchased from a supermarket, while fried chicken from a food vendor has less saturated and trans fats than a well-known supermarket brand.[23] This suggests that food vendors know how to prepare chicken better than doughnuts.

Campaigns to clean up the streets of Singapore, Penang, Hanoi, and Bangkok stressed the need for sanitary foods and hygienic preparation techniques. Food vendors were often gathered into locations where they could be more easily regulated; vendors had to be certified, licensed, and carefully scrutinized by public health officials. As a result, food vendors in many cities are required to wear rubber gloves, use bottled water, and arrange to have a source of hot water for washing dishes. Those who conform to these standards might receive a seal of approval as a vender of "safe" street foods. However, efforts to remove street vendors were also about trying to create a cleaner, more modern streetscape, more characteristic of Euro-American cities.

DIETARY GLOBALIZATION

Dairy products are not the only European foods that have been absorbed into Southeast Asian diets. Changes in food habits and food availability are responsible for the modern "toxic food environment," according to media reports in Malaysia and Thailand. Climbing obesity rates are blamed on western fast food chains. Problematic foods are identified as those high in salt, sugar, and fat, and include instant noodles, deep-fried chicken, pizzas, hamburgers, french fries, doughnuts, cookies, and cakes. These "mouth-watering edibles" are found everywhere, leading to increasing rates of coronary heart disease, diabetes, hypertension, and to some extent, cancer. Heart disease and cancer, diseases of the affluent, are now the primary causes of death in Thailand. Half the Thai population over 60 suffers from hypertension and the diabetes rate in Thailand is even higher than in EU countries.[24]

For most of Southeast Asia, food security (quantity) concerns have been replaced by concerns about food safety (quality and sustainability). And improvements in food safety are as much about trade as health. For example, New York City's ban on trans fats has "trickled down" to other countries, as consumers add concerns about trans fats to concerns about calories and cholesterol. Companies in Southeast Asia that export foods to North America are now testing for trans fats to meet FDA labeling requirements. Packages of instant red, yellow, and green curry pastes are considered at risk for trans fats and saturated fats, but they are more likely to be packaged for export than used locally where wet markets provide a wide range of fresh flavor pastes for purchase.[25]

Western foods and fast food chains are often blamed for changes in food consumption patterns. But western-style fast food restaurants in the cities of Southeast Asia are more appreciated for their air-conditioning and clean bathrooms than the taste of their food offerings, and are more popular among teenagers than adults.[26] Nor are these changes in food-consumption practices simply the result of changing tastes among the Thai or Malaysian public. The Thai government, for example, favored companies that reduced the costs of meats, fats, oils, and sugars. Now powerful businesses in these sectors are increasing their profits by producing ever-cheaper and poorer-quality foods, meals, snacks, and drinks.[27]

In the modern cities of Malaysia, rising obesity rates have also replaced problems of undernutrition. Some attribute this to the "rubbish foods" appearing in school cafeterias where hot dogs and cakes have replaced rice and bananas. Obesity rates for children and adults are doubling every few years in some parts of the world. Food insecure countries without access to western foods and fast food chains are also adversely affected by trade. The smallest markets in the uplands of Burma, Thailand, Lao PDR, and Vietnam sell candies and cakes, along with small packets of infant formula, all imported or smuggled in from China. School vendors who used to sell bananas and fruit to schoolchildren now offer them these cheap processed foods.

Food vendors making doughnuts in Salaya, Thailand, 2008.

But this experience of modernity and the fear of toxic modern foods is countered by an equally strong counter process. New consumer demands for healthy foods—clean, organic, and sustainable—are encouraging the development of a new range of products. Thailand wants to be the "Kitchen of the World," but ranks 13th in Asia among organic food producers. Yet demand for organic food is rising rapidly in parts of Southeast Asia, as elsewhere in the world.[28] Retailers double the price of organic produce because they know that the urban middle class and elites will pay the price. However, much of the produce labeled organic is really grown conventionally. Other organic foods such as asparagus are shipped directly to niche markets in Europe.

HEALTHY CUISINES

In spite of food scares, malnourished infants, and overweight adults, Southeast Asian cuisines, in addition to being tasty, are overwhelmingly healthy. There are few food cultures more ideally suited to human health than those based on rice, fish, fresh vegetables, and fruit. What makes Southeast Asian food cultures among the healthiest and most appealing in the world? Their experimental approaches to new tastes; an ethos of moderation and the middle way; high standards of personal and kitchen hygiene; an emphasis on contrasting flavors rather than supersized portions; a preference for fresh rather than processed ingredients; and meal formats that allow meals and mouthfuls to be individualized and personalized. All these valuable traits show a unique approach to food. Throughout Southeast Asia, in the villages and cities, people take intense pride in local ingredients and have a willingness to experiment with someone else's local and make it their own—a truly global approach to food and eating.

NOTES

1. The botanical gardens in Leiden were founded by the great Dutch physician, Hermann Boerhaave, and contain *materia medica* from Java. See L. S. King, *The Medical World of the Eighteenth Century* (Chicago: University of Chicago Press, 1958).

2. Carol Laderman, *Wives and Midwives: Childbirth and Nutrition in Rural Malaysia* (Berkeley, CA: University of California Press, 1983), p. 59.

3. J. Mulholland, *Medicine, Magic, and Evil Spirits*, monograph 8 (Canberra: Faculty of Asian Studies, Australia National University, 1987), p. 20.

4. An exception to this is Hindu Bali; here some elements of caste were adapted, particularly those related to religious rituals.

5. The award-winning book by Anne Fadiman, *The Spirit Catches You and You Fall Down* (New York: Farrar, Strauss, and Giroux, 1997), captures the agony of this Hmong family in California as they and the doctors tried to make sense of each other's explanations for disease.

6. The logic of taste refers back to the Sanskrit term *rasa* and can be expanded to apply to emotions and beauty as well as food. The expanded meanings derived from the Sanskrit term *rasa* need more research. The separation of the categories of food, cosmetics, and drugs into separate categories does little to explain taste in the Inndianized regions of Southeast Asia where these categories fit more on a single continuum.

7. There is a substantial literature on reproductive health and diet in Southeast Asia. These ethnographic studies apply to local communities and are difficult to compare. See, for example, Laderman, *Wives and Midwives.*

8. This list comes from a handwritten document in the William Sage collection on Laos at Arizona State Library.

9. I. Delforge, "Laos at the Crossroads," *Seedling* 18 (2001).

10. For a more in-depth comparison between mainland (Thai) and island (Java) herbal treatments, see Penny Van Esterik, "To Strengthen and Refresh: Herbal Therapy in Southeast Asia," *Social Science and Medicine* 27, no. 8 (1988): 751–759.

11. "A Balanced Way of Eating," *Bangkok Post*, January 13, 2008.

12. *Agriculture and Rural Development for Reducing Hunger in Asia* (Washington, DC: IFPRI, 2007), p. 2.

13. *Malnutrition Worldwide* (Rome: World Health Organization, 1998).

14. *Report on Food Insecurity in Laos Released, Press Release* (Vientiane, Lao PDR, October 12, 2007). Child-health statistics are all from UNICEF country profiles.

15. Jutta Krahn, "The Dynamics of Dietary Change of Transitional Food Systems in Tropical Forest Areas of Southeast Asia: The Contemporary and Traditional Food System of the Katu in the Sekong Province, Lao PDR" (dissertation, Rheinische Friedrich-Wildhelms Univeritaet, 2005), p. 43.

16. Luis Ramirez, "Burma's Control of Transportation System Causes Millions to Go Hungry," VOA, Bangkok, January 9, 2008.

17. N. Minot, et al., "Income Diversification and Poverty in the Northern Uplands of Vietnam" (research report 145, Washington, DC, IFPRI, 2006).

18. H. Waters, et al., "Weight-for-Age Malnutrition in Indonesian Children, 1992–1999," *International Journal of Epidemiology* 33, no. 3 (2004): 589–595.

19. "Overnutrition: A Growing Concern," *Bangkok Post*, January 6, 2008, p. 12.

20. "'Good Nutrition Key to the Solution' Assert Nations as They Strive to Fight HIV/AIDS and Malnutrition in South-East Asia," WHO South-East Asia regional office press release, Bangkok, October 8, 2007.

21. A. Den Hartog, "Acceptance of Milk Products in Southeast Asia," in *Asian Food: The Global and the Local,* ed. K. Cwiertka (Richmond, Surrey, UK: Curzon, 2002), pp. 34–45. See also Penny Van Esterik, "Sweetened

Condensed Soma: Dietary Innovation in Southeast Asia," *Filipinas* 1, no. 1 (1980): 96–102.

22. Thanes Wongyannava, in *The Transformation of Chinese Haute Cuisine in Bangkok's Chinese Restaurants* (research report, Toyoto Foundation, 2001), p. 72, argues that the rapid disappearance of beef-based dishes in Thailand after 2000 was linked to the rise of the cult of Kwan Yin, whose followers do not eat beef, rather than fears about mad cow disease.

23. *Situational Survey on Trans Fatty Acids Contamination in Food Products in Thailand* (2550 Salaya, Mahidol University), p. 41 (in Thai).

24. "Overnutrition: A Growing Concern," p. 12.

25. Linda Leake, "Trans Fats to Go," *Food Technology* 61, no. 2 (2007): 66–67.

26. See, for example, J. Watson, *Golden Arches East: McDonald's in East Asia* (Stanford: Stanford University Press, 1997), or Yun Xiang Yan, "Of Hamburgers and Social Space: Consuming McDonald's in Beijing," in *Food and Culture: A Reader*, 2nd ed., ed. C. Counihan and Penny Van Esterik (New York: Routledge Press, 2008).

27. Siriporn Sachamuneewongee, "Over-nutrition, a Growing Concern," *Bangkok Post*, January 6, 2008, p. 12.

28. Petchanet Pratruangkrai, "Organic Food Exports to Soar," *Nation*, January 11, 2008.

Glossary

Acar pickles   Relishes or chutneys.

Adat   Customary law in Malaysia and Indonesia.

Animism   A belief in spirits.

Cardamom   A relative of ginger, the pod is used in Cambodian, Malaysian, and Vietnamese dishes.

Cinnamon or cassia bark   Usually sold in sticks or ground to a powder and used in Malaysian and Indonesian dishes.

Cloves   Small black flower buds of a plant found in the Spice Islands, the Moluccas. The plant has medicinal properties and is common in Malaysian and Indonesian food.

Commensality   Eating together, sharing food.

Coriander   Leaves, stems, seeds, and roots are all used. The seeds are usually ground, while the leaves and stems are popular in a wide range of dishes. The roots are important in Thai-Lao cooking. A long-leafed version with a serrated edge is used in Vietnamese and Cambodian soups and eaten raw in northeast Thai-Lao dishes.

Curry Powder   A commercial product originally developed by the British to imitate the dried spice mixtures (masala) used in Indian cooking. Local mixtures are used in Burmese and Malaysian cooking.

Devaraja   A god-king in the Indianized kingdoms of Southeast Asia.

Dongson   A Neolithic ritual complex that made large bronze drums.

Galangal   A relative of ginger used in soups and curries in Thai, Lao, Khmer, Vietnamese, and Indonesian cooking (where it is known as *laos*).

Ginger   Tuber grown throughout Southeast Asia that has medicinal properties and is often used to make a healing hot tea.

Halal   An Arabic term meaning lawful or allowed food.

Hari Raya   Festival in Malaysia and Indonesia marking the end of Ramadan.

Hoabinhian   Prehistoric hunter-gatherers of mainland Southeast Asia.

Indianization   The influence of India on religion and politics, including adding Hindu-Buddhist rituals to create divine kingship.

Jamu   Javanese herbal medicine taken to enhance health, beauty, and sexual appeal.

Laolao   Rice alcohol.

Lemongrass   An herb native to Malaysia. The tough stalks provide a popular flavor in soups and can be ground in Thai, Lao, Khmer, Vietnamese, Malaysian, and Indonesian flavor pastes.

Mace   The membrane on the nutmeg, usually sold in powder form.

Mint   Aromatic herb used fresh in Lao and Vietnamese salads and in meat dishes.

Nats   Burmese spirits or supernatural beings.

Nutmeg   A valuable spice from the Spice Islands, the Moluccas. It is grated into many Malaysian and Indonesian dishes.

Nyonya   Malay and Chinese hybrid cuisine.

Padek/Prahok   Term for fermented fish products in Lao and Cambodian.

Pandanus Leaves   Provide flavor to steamed dishes and are used as wrappers and plates.

Pat Thai   Thai fried noodle dish.

Pho   Vietnamese noodle soup.

Ramadan   Period of Muslim fasting.

Rijstaffel   Dutch rice table meal composed of Indonesian dishes.

Sakhan   An aromatic wood used in Luang Prabang, Lao PDR, to provide a distinctive bitter taste to stews.

Santi Asoke   A reformist Buddhist sect in Thailand known for vegetarianism, meditation practices, and claims about simple living. It has developed its own monkhood, which is of concern to orthodox Theravada Buddhists.

Satay   Grilled meat on a stick.

Shallot   A variety of small red onion used in flavor pastes and stir-fry dishes.

Slametan   A ritual commensal meal most common in Java.

Star Anise   A star-shaped spice used whole in Vietnamese cooking, particularly in making *pho* soup.

Tamarind   Often used in the form of a paste made from the tamarind pod dissolved in water, it gives a sour taste to soups and stews. Pods are obtained from wild and cultivated trees. Both leaves and flowers are eaten. Tamarind plants have a long history of medicinal use as an astringent, laxative, and to lower blood pressure.

Tet   Tet Nguyen Dan, the Vietnamese New Year.

Theravada Buddhism   "Teaching of the Elders." A community-based religion practiced primarily in Burma, Thailand, Lao PDR, and Cambodia, also referred to as Hinayana Buddhism.

Turmeric   A root related to ginger, it gives a yellow color to dishes. It is common in Burma, Malaysia and Indonesia, and also has medicinal uses as an antiseptic.

Wild Lime   Also known as kaffir lime. The fruit and wild lime leaves are used to flavor curries and soups.

Resource Guide

SUGGESTED READING

There are several outstanding cookbooks that examine food systems across the whole region of Southeast Asia. Rosemary Brissenden's 2007 edition of *Southeast Asian Food* provides cultural background and recipes from Indonesia, Malaysia, Singapore, Thailand, Laos, Cambodia, and Vietnam. Jeffrey Alford and Naomi Duguid's journey along the Mekong River, *Hot Sour Salty Sweet* (2000), shows culinary connections between meals in the Yunnan province of southern China, and those in Thailand, Lao PDR, Cambodia, and Vietnam. Earlier books such as Maudie Horsting and others' *Flavors of Southeast Asia: Recipes from Indonesia, Thailand, and Vietnam* (1979) also attempt comparison between national cuisines.

Because Alan Davidson's career took him to many Southeast Asian countries, his *Oxford Companion to Food* (1999) is a treasure trove of information about the region. Some of his best pieces are published in his 1990 anthology, *A Kipper with My Tea*. He is also responsible for bringing the best-known books on Lao food to publication, including having the book of recipes by Phia Sing from the royal palace in Luang Prabang published as *Traditional Recipes of Laos* (1981), as well as his 1975 book *Fish and Fish Dishes of Laos*. Daovone Xayavong's *Taste of Laos* (2000) and Penn Hongthong's *Simple Laotian Cooking* (2003) provide detailed recipes from an insider's perspective. In contrast, Natacha Du Pont De Bie describes her adventures as a food tourist in Lao PDR with fewer recipes, but lots of local color, in *Ant Egg Soup* (2004).

There are few books in English that examine food systems historically in the region, but many cookbooks geared to western cooks. Most of this literature focuses on Thailand, beginning with Marie Wilson's *Siamese Cookery* (1965) and Jennifer Brennan's *The Original Thai Cookbook* (1981). Malulee Pinsuvana 's several volumes of *Cooking Thai Food in American Kitchens* are very useful, particularly book 3, which comes with instructions and a set of tools for fruit and vegetable carving.

Most of what is known about the history of Thai cuisine is cited in David Thompson's mammoth book, *Thai Food* (2002). He provides detailed information on dishes that come directly from Thai sources. The most striking fact about many Thai cookbooks is their beauty. Food and settings are photographed with an artist's eye in the Heritage Edition of *Thailand: The Beautiful Cookbook* (1992), edited by William Warren. Other excellent choices include the National Identity Board of Thailand's publication *Thai Life: Thai Cuisine* (1986), M. L. Taw Kritakara and M. R. Pimsai Amranand's *Modern Thai Cooking* (1977), Vatcharin Bhumichitr's *The Taste of Thailand* (1988), and all Wandee Na Songkhla's books on royal Thai cuisine. For food tourists, *Thai Hawker Food* (2001) is indispensable, as it locates some of the more obscure food vendors and identifies their specialties.

For Burma, Susan Chan's *Flavors of Burma* provides easy-to-follow recipes along with cultural background, as does Aung Aung Taik's 1993 book, *Under the Golden Pagoda: The Best of Burmese Cooking*. The *Elephant Walk Cookbook*, by Longteine de Monteiro and Katherine Neustadt (1998), is a wonderful introduction to Cambodian culture and food. Similarly, Vietnamese cuisine is becoming better known through the work of Andrea Nguyen, with *Into the Vietnamese Kitchen* (2006) and related websites. Nongkran Daks and Alexandra Greeley's *Homestyle Vietnamese Cooking* (2002) includes recipes for the best-known Vietnamese dishes.

The islands are not the focus of this book, but books like *The Cradle of Flavor: Home Cooking from the Spice Islands of Indonesia, Malaysia, and Singapore*, by James Oseland (2006), illustrate the many linkages between the flavors of the mainland and the islands. Cecelia Tan's *Penang Nyonya Cooking: Foods of My Childhood* (1983) brings the connections between Chinese and Malay cooking into perspective. This book has only occasionally touched on food of the Philippines. However, there are excellent resources available on this country, notably Amy Besa and Rory Dorotan's *Memories of Philippine Kitchens* (2006).

WEB SITES

There are many sites and blogs that provide recipes for Southeast Asian dishes, particularly Thai and Malaysian food. The following sites are primarily in English.

Lao Cuisine. http://www.laocuisine.net. Discusses recipes and offers a nostalgic look at foods no longer available to Lao in North America, Europe, or Australia.

Malaysian Food. http://www.malaysianfood.net. A range of Malay and Nyonya recipes, and a useful glossary of Malay food.

Rasa Malaysia. http://www.rasamalaysia.com. Covers the range of foods offered in Malaysia.

Royal Thai Cuisine. http://www.royalthai-cuisine.com. Promotes restaurants that offer royal-style palace cooking.

Streetfood: Serving up Streetfood in the Global South. http://www.streetfood.org. A site devoted to the preservation of street foods, worldwide.

Temple of Thai. http://templeofthai.com. A good range of Thai recipes.

Wandering Spoon. http://www.wanderingspoon.com. A particular focus on Vietnamese food.

Selected Bibliography

Alford, Jeffrey, and Naomi Duguid. *Hot Sour Salty Sweet*. Toronto: Random House Canada, 2000.

———. *Seductions of Rice*. New York: Artisan Press, 1998.

Avieli, Nir. "Rice Talks: A Culinary Ethnography of Identity and Change in Hoi An, Central Vietnam." PhD Thesis, Hebrew University, 2003.

Benda, Harry, and John Larkin. *The World of Southeast Asia: Selected Historical Readings*. New York: Harper and Row, 1967.

Besa, Amy, and Rory Dorotan. *Memories of Philippine Kitchens*. New York: Steward, Tabori, and Chang, 2006.

Brennan, Jennifer. *The Original Thai Cookbook*. New York: Coward, McCann, and Geoghegan, 1981.

Brissenden, Rosemary. *Southeast Asian Food*. Singapore: Periplus Editions, 2007.

Chan, Susan. *Flavors of Burma: Myanmar: Cuisine and Culture from the Land of the Golden Pagodas*. New York: Hippocrene Books, 2003.

Cheung, Sidney, and Tan Chee-Beng, eds. *Food and Foodways in Asia: Resource, Tradition, and Cooking*. New York: Routledge, 2007.

Coedes, George. *The Indianized States of Southeast Asia*. Honolulu: University of Hawaii Press, 1968.

Counihan, Carole, and Penny Van Esterik, eds. *Food and Culture: A Reader*. 2nd ed. New York: Routledge, 2008.

Daks, Nongkran, and Alexandra Greeley. *Homestyle Vietnamese Cooking*. Singapore: Periplus Editions, 2002.

Daovone Xayavong. *Taste of Laos*. Berkeley, CA: SLG Books, 2000.

Davidson, Alan. *Fish and Fish Dishes of Laos*. Rutland, VT: Charles E. Tuttle, 1975.

————. *A Kipper with my Tea*. San Francisco: North Point Press, 1990.

————. *The Oxford Companion to Food*. Oxford: Oxford University Press, 1999.

De Monteiro, Longteine, and Katherine Neustadt. *The Elephant Walk Cookbook*. Boston: Houghton Mifflin, 1998.

Du Pont De Bie, Natacha. *Ant Egg Soup: The Adventures of a Food Tourist in Laos*. London: Hodder and Stoughton, 2004.

Greeley, Alexandra. *Asian Grills*. New York: Doubleday, 1993.

Hamilton, Roy. *The Art of Rice*. Los Angeles: UCLA Fowler Museum of Cultural History, 2003.

Hanks, Lucien. *Rice and Man*. Chicago: Aldine-Atherton, 1972.

Heldke, Lisa. *Exotic Appetites*. New York: Routledge, 2003.

Ho, Alice Yen. *At the South-East Asian Table*. Singapore: Oxford University Press, 1995.

Penn Hongthong. *Simple Laotian Cooking*. New York: Hippocrene Books, 2003.

Horsting, Maudie, et al. *Flavors of Southeast Asia: Recipes from Indonesia, Thailand, and Vietnam*. San Francisco: 101 Productions, 1979.

Hutton, Wendy, ed. *The Food of Thailand: Authentic Recipes from the Golden Kingdom*. Singapore: Periplus Editions, 1995.

Hyman, Gwenda. *Cuisines of Southeast Asia*. New York: John Wiley, 1995.

Ireson-Doolittlle, C., and G. Moreno-Black. *The Lao: Gender, Power, and Livelihood*. Boulder: Westview Press, 2004.

Jacquat, Christiane. *Plants from the Markets of Thailand*. Bangkok: DK Books, 1990.

Janowski, Monica, and F. Kerlogue, eds., *Kinship and Food in South East Asia*. Copenhagen: NIAS Press, 2007.

Kanit Muntarbhorn. *Gastronomy in Asia*. Bk. 1. Bangkok: M. T. Press, 2007.

Krahn, Jutta. "The Dynamics of Dietary Change of Transitional Food Systems in Tropical Forest Areas of Southeast Asia: The Contemporary and Traditional Food System of the Katu in the Sekong Province, Lao PDR." Diss., Rheinische Friedrich-Wildhelms Univeritaet, 2005.

Laderman, Carol. *Wives and Midwives: Childbirth and Nutrition in Rural Malaysia*. Berkeley, CA: University of California Press, 1983.

Malulee Pinsuvana. *Cooking Thai Food in American Kitchens*. 3rd ed. Bangkok: Sahamitr Industrial Printing, 1979.

————. *Cooking Thai Food in American Kitchens*. Bk. 3, *With Garnish and Entertaining*. Bangkok: Thai Watana Panich Press Co., Ltd., 1993.

Michaud, Jean. *Turbulent Times and Enduring Peoples: Mountain Minorities in the Southeast Asian Massif*. Richmond, Surrey: Curzon, 2000.

National Identity Board of Thailand. *Thai Life: Thai Cuisine*. Bangkok: Prime Minister's Office, 1986.

Nguyen, Andrea. *Into the Vietnamese Kitchen*. Berkeley, CA: Ten Speed Press, 2006.

Osborne, Milton. *Southeast Asia: An Introductory History*. 8th ed. St. Leonards, Australia: Allen & Unwin, 2000.

Oseland, James. *Cradle of Flavor: Home Cooking from the Spice Islands of Indonesia, Malaysia, and Singapore*. New York: W. W. Norton & Company, 2006.

Phia Sing. *Traditional Recipes of Laos*. London: Prospect Books, 1981.

Reichart, P., and H. Philipsen. *Betel and Miang: Vanishing Thai Habits*. Bangkok: White Lotus, 2005.

Reid, Anthony. *Southeast Asia in the Age of Commerce (1450–1680)*. Vol. 1, *The Land Below the Winds*. New Haven: Yale University Press, 1988.

Scupin, R. *Peoples and Cultures of Asia*. Upper Saddle River, NJ: Prentice Hall, 2006.

Sesser, Stan. *The Lands of Charm and Cruelty: Travels in Southeast Asia*. New York: Knopf, 1993.

Spiro, Melford. *Buddhism and Society*. New York: Harper and Row, 1970.

Taik, Aung Aung. *Under the Golden Pagoda: The Best of Burmese Cooking*. San Francisco: Chronicle Books, 1993.

Tan, Cecelia. *Penang Nyonya Cooking: Foods of My Childhood*. Singapore: Time Books International, 1983.

Tanaka, Yoshitaka, and Nguyen Van Ke. *Edible Wild Plants of Vietnam*. Bangkok: Orchid Press, 2007.

Taw Kritakara, M. L., and M. R. Pimsai Amranand. *Modern Thai Cooking*. Bangkok: Editions Duang Kamol, 1977.

Thompson, David. *Thai Food*. Berkeley, CA: Ten Speed Press, 2002.

Trankell, Ing-Britt. "Cooking, Care, and Domestication: A Culinary Ethnography of the Tai Yong, Northern Thailand." *Uppsala Studies in Cultural Anthropology* 21 (1995).

Turner, Jack. *Spice: The History of a Temptation*. New York: Vintage Books, 2004.

Van Esterik, Penny. "Anna and the King: Digesting Difference." *Southeast Asian Research* 14, no. 2 (2006): 289–307.

———. "Food and the Refugee Experience: Gender and Food in Exile, Asylum, and Repatriation." In *Development and Diaspora*, ed. W. Giles, H. Moussa, and P. Van Esterik. Dundas, Ontario: Artemis Press, 1996.

———. "From Hunger Foods to Heritage Foods: Challenges to Food Localization in Lao PDR." In *Slow Food/Fast Food: The Cultural Economy of the Global Food System*, ed. R. Wilk. Lanham, MD: Altamira Press, 2006.

———. "From Marco Polo to McDonald's: Thai Cuisine in Transition." *Food and Foodways* 5, no. 2 (1992): 177–193.

———. *Materializing Thailand*. Oxford: Berg Press, 2000.

———. *Taking Refuge: Lao Buddhists in North America*. Tempe, AZ: Program for Southeast Asian Studies, Arizona State University, 2003.

———. *Women of Southeast Asia*. Southeast Asia Monograph Series. DeKalb, IL: Northern Illinois University, first published 1982, republished 1996.

Vatcharin Bhumichitr. *The Taste of Thailand*. London: Pavilion Books, 1988.

Wandee Na Songkhla. *The Royal Favourite Dishes*. Bangkok. 1977.

———. *Royal Thai Cuisine*. Bk. 1. Bangkok. 1980.

Warren, William, ed. *Thailand: The Beautiful Cookbook*. Heritage Edition. Bangkok: Asia Books, 1992.

Wilson, Marie. *Siamese Cookery*. Rutland, VT: Charles E. Tuttle, 1965.

Wolters, O. W. *History, Culture, and Region in Southeast Asian Perspectives*. Singapore: Institute of Southeast Asian Studies, 1982.

Yasmeen, Gisele. *Bangkok's Foodscape: Public Eating, Gender Relations, and Urban Change*. Bangkok: White Lotus, 2006.

Index

About the Author

PENNY VAN ESTERIK is Professor of Anthropology at York University and has specialized in Southeast Asia. She is a noted expert on food and nutrition in the region and has authored and edited a number of works, including *Food and Culture: A Reader* (1997).

Recent Titles in
Food Culture around the World